```
LB
3044      Beatty, LaMond F.
 .B43         Instructional materials
          centers.
```

INSTRUCTIONAL MATERIALS CENTERS

The Instructional Media Library

Volume Number 5

INSTRUCTIONAL MATERIALS CENTERS

LaMond F. Beatty
Educational Systems and Learning Resources
University of Utah

James E. Duane
Series Editor

**Educational Technology Publications
Englewood Cliffs, New Jersey 07632**

Library of Congress Cataloging in Publication Data

Beatty, LaMond F
    Instructional materials centers.

    (The Instructional media library ; v. no. 5)
    Bibliography: p.
    1. Instructional materials centers. I. Title.
II. Series: Instructional media library ; v. no. 5.
LB3044.B43   371.6'21   80-21451
ISBN 0-87778-165-6

Copyright © 1981 Educational Technology Publications, Inc., Englewood Cliffs, New Jersey 07632.

All rights reserved. No part of this book may be reproduced or transmitted, in any form or by any means, electronic or mechanical, including photocopying, recording, or by any information storage and retrieval system, without permission in writing from the Publisher.

Printed in the United States of America.

Library of Congress Catalog Card Number: 80-21451

International Standard Book Number: 0-87778-165-6

First Printing: January, 1981.

Table of Contents

1. Introduction 3
2. Description of Instructional Materials Centers 7
3. Objectives of This Book 9
4. Characteristics of Instructional Materials Centers ... 11
5. Utilization of the Center 13
6. Design of the Center 37
7. Case Studies 69
8. Future Trends 72
9. Suggested Reader Project Activities 74
10. Glossary of Terms 76
11. Software Producers 81
12. Hardware Producers 84
13. Bibliography 88

INSTRUCTIONAL MATERIALS CENTERS

1.
Introduction

Information processing is not something done only through modern, technological methods; it is as old as man. Man's earliest system for storing information and transmitting it from one person to another was the spoken language. Using words, ritual, stories, prayer, etc., man passed from one generation to another knowledge of progress and achievements.

Early in man's history, it was realized that spoken words could be represented by visual symbols. With this discovery, man invented the second great means for the preservation and transmission of knowledge—writing—a medium used for over 5,000 years.

The library became the instrumentality of society to store written records so that they could be protected and preserved and made available for use when needed. Throughout man's recorded history, great libraries have been established to store, protect, and preserve written knowledge. Much of what we know about ancient civilizations comes from the wealth of knowledge stored in libraries. Knowledge of the Babylonian civilization comes from the tablets of the Library of Borsippa, which were copied and preserved in the library of King Ashurbanipal of Assyria (668-626 B.C.). The great library of Ramses II of Egypt, located at Thebes (1250 B.C.), is believed to have contained twenty thousand books.

The most important libraries of ancient Greece were established during the Hellenistic Age. These great libraries were located at Alexandria in Egypt and in the Kingdom of Pergamum in Asia Minor. The libraries became the repository of manuscripts containing the highest form of literary creativity known to man: the tragedies of Sophocles and Euripides; the lyric poetry of Pindar; the histories of Thucydides and Herodotus; the comedies of Aristophanes; the philosophy of Socrates; as well as the thoughts of mankind in the subjects of science, religion, politics, law, architecture, art, history, and mathematics.

Greek influence over the cultural and intellectual life of the Roman people began in 272 B.C., and by the time of the Roman conquest of Greece in 146 B.C., the Romans had read and studied Greek literature, philosophy, science, history, and mathematics. Private libraries became an important feature of Roman civilization when generals began to return from conquests with entire libraries among their spoils of war. As a significant part of Rome's civilizing process, libraries spread through Italy, Greece, Asia Minor, Cyprus, and Africa.

The Christian monastic movement was responsible for the preservation and continuation of the recorded history of Western civilization. It kept alive after the fall of Rome the scholarly activities of Western civilization.

The rise of Cathedral schools, the study of Latin, the appearance of the written word in the language of the masses, and an increasingly favorable social and economic condition gave rise to great universities during the Middle Ages. These outstanding universities—at Bologna, Paris, Prague, Heidelberg, Oxford, and Cambridge—established libraries for the use of students and educated patrons. These universities spurred on the revival of the study of Greek and Latin literature and helped to usher in the Renaissance.

The discovery of the Americas was one of the achieve-

Introduction 5

ments of the Renaissance, with the renewed hopes of mankind for religious and intellectual freedom. The English colonists came to the New World to start a new life and with them came one of their most cherished of possessions—books. The early colleges and universities in the Colonies began with endowments of books to start libraries. Before the American Revolution, nine colleges were established in the Colonies. By the period of 1868 (the Civil War), more than 500 colleges and universities had been established, all with libraries housing books and other means of transmitting man's recorded knowledge.

Additional methods of transmitting knowledge—other than books—have been associated with education since antiquity. While books have been the most common medium, many other instructional materials have been used. Aristotle used the "Camera Obscura" (an optical device which forms a visible image of an external scene inside a darkened box) as a teaching device for instructing his students at the Lyceum in 330 B.C. Anatomical drawings done with careful scientific accuracy and displayed as flip charts, wall charts, and posters were used at the University of Padua as early as 1543 A.D. The "magic lantern" (the first slide projector, used to project still pictures, using sunlight at first, then oil, gas, and finally electricity as a source of illumination) was invented in Germany around 1870 and was used in universities in Germany, Italy, Ireland, and the United States of America only a few years later.

The desire to make pictures move led to vigorous research efforts following the demonstration of a prototype motion picture projection system by Thomas Edison in 1894. Prior to this demonstration, a host of gadgets, including peep-hole devices, revolving drums, flipping cards, and other devices designed to enable the viewer to see pictures that presented the appearance of movement, had been used as instructional devices in schools and colleges throughout Europe and the

United States. Edison's system to record and transmit man's spoken words via discs (records) also saw early use in schools, colleges, and universities.

Since World War II, new instructional materials have appeared. These have included programmed instruction and teaching machines, television, language laboratories, and computer-assisted instruction.

The appearance of these many additional resources for instruction and learning has brought about a new role for the traditional library. Beginning in the 1960's, the library began to become an instructional materials center (IMC), providing facilities for cataloging, storing, and disseminating information available in varied forms.

This new library has also grown to include the acquisition, maintenance, and distribution of all kinds of machines needed to project, play, or display the varied instructional materials.

The Federal Government, through such laws as the National Defense Education Act, the Elementary and Secondary Education Act, the Higher Education Facilities Act, and Public Law 94-142, which guarantees an appropriate education for all handicapped children, has provided funds for the establishment and maintenance of instructional materials centers in schools, colleges, and universities throughout the United States.

The traditional role of the library as a repository for books in a book-oriented society has changed. A new role has emerged. Today the instructional materials center is at the heart of a diversified instructional program. It is an important factor in the development of each learner's potential.

2.
Description of Instructional Materials Centers

The instructional materials center has developed into a comprehensive media-service program that has grown out of an expanded concept of the library function. The instructional materials center provides a learning environment for students and teachers, including easily accessible sources of all types of instructional materials in varied formats. The instructional materials center is not merely a single-stop place where one picks up materials; it is also a place for learning. It provides study spaces for individual viewing and listening, small-group discussion, quiet reading, and audio-visual production.

In the instructional materials center, all learning materials have equal status and receive due consideration. The collection will contain the whole range of instructional materials used in the teaching and learning process. Printed matter (books, pamphlets, newspapers, and periodicals) and audio and visual materials (slides, filmstrips, overhead transparencies, audio- and videotapes, records, realia, and the equipment needed to use them) are equally available to teachers, students, and administrators. Free and inexpensive materials, charts, maps and globes, models, specimens, dioramas, lists for field trip excursions, and resource speakers from the community are available. Individualized instructional packages/modules and assistance in computerized instruction may also be on hand in the IMC.

The instructional materials center is defined, then, in terms of its several functions—circulation, coordination, inservice education, consultation, and local production of materials. All types of instructional materials are circulated from and used within the center. The use and selection of these instructional materials are coordinated with radio and television programs. Consultation services are available for students, teachers, and administrators to provide the best resources available to help solve particular learning and teaching problems. A wide variety of instructional materials is produced within the instructional materials center to supplement commercially available materials or to provide instructional resources of a specific local nature. These locally produced instructional materials may be as diverse as a chart, a mounted still picture, a series of 35mm color slides, a graphic for a televised program, an overhead transparency, or a computer-assisted instruction module.

The instructional materials center, then, provides the support needed to insure that the curricular endeavors of the school are met.

3.
Objectives of This Book

After completing this book, the reader will be able to:
- Describe the basic differences between a library and an instructional materials center.
- List and describe factors that have influenced the evolution of the "traditional" library from a facility that contained mainly books to a center that provides information in all formats.
- List and describe the units that constitute the basic or fundamental spaces of an instructional materials center.
- List and describe the units that constitute the supplemental spaces of an instructional materials center.
- Indicate the minimum square footage recommended for each of the units in the "basic" and "supplemental" spaces of an instructional materials center.
- List national and local authorities for the recommendations of minimum space allocations and square footage requirements for an instructional materials center.
- Describe the interrelatedness of all of the units that constitute the instructional materials center.
- Describe the factors that insure a smooth flow of traffic within the instructional materials center.
- Describe the factors that must be considered in each of the following areas when planning the instructional materials center: lighting, acoustical treatment, floor coverings,

electrical power availability, wall treatments, and color schemes.
- List several commercial firms that produce hardware needed to furnish an instructional materials center.
- List several commercial firms that produce student study carrels.
- Describe what is meant by individualized instruction and list and describe types of individualized instructional programs.
- List and describe the major "circulation" services provided by the IMC.
- List and describe the major "reference" services provided within the IMC.
- List and describe the "production" functions performed in or by the staff of the IMC.
- List and describe the types of activities that students engage in within the environment of the IMC.
- List and describe "teacher" activities that can be performed or utilized within the programs, services, or confines of the IMC.
- List and describe the "basic" items that constitute a *collection* of instructional materials needed for a 1,000 student-population instructional materials center.
- List and describe the "basic" items that constitute the *equipment* needed for a 1,000 student-population instructional materials center.
- List and describe how the *media specialist* provides assistance to teachers.
- List and describe the services that a *media technician* provides teachers.
- List and describe the elements of a *systematic* approach to the development of learning sequences.
- List and describe, in detail, the five phases needed to implement a total system of instruction, including some suggestions for specific instructional materials and equipment that will assist in each phase.

4.
Characteristics of Instructional Materials Centers

1. An instructional materials center is composed of leadership and staff personnel, equipment, materials, and facilities.
2. Savings can be made by providing a special structure or space for the instructional materials center. Special features, such as requirements for high ceilings in television studios, sophisticated electronics systems, and acoustical treatment of many areas, can be accommodated with a great overall savings in construction by concentrating these facilities in one area (the IMC) rather than in many small spaces throughout the building.
3. The instructional materials center provides a learning environment for students, teachers, and administrators. It is an easily accessible source of materials—books, pamphlets, documents, periodicals, maps, charts, posters, realia, films, filmstrips, slides, overhead transparencies, videotapes, etc.
4. The instructional materials center provides the facilities to help the individual school maintain a sense of coherence. Departments, teachers, and administrators have a unifying agency that brings together individual efforts to form a unified whole.
5. The instructional materials center provides the trained staff, evaluation instruments, and centralized facilities needed

to evaluate the effectiveness and excellence of teaching and learning in the school.

6. The instructional materials center makes available to the teaching faculty all media, technology, services, and systems which will enhance the effective communication of ideas in the presentation phase of learning.

7. The instructional materials center makes available to students all media, technology, services, and systems which will enhance the effective communication of ideas in the self-programmed phases of learning.

8. The instructional materials center—with a centralized instructional materials program, staff, and facility—serves the objectives of the total educational program by:

   (a) locating, collecting, organizing, promoting, and distributing learning resources for use by teachers and students as individuals and groups;
   (b) providing leadership in utilization, motivation, experimentation, and evaluation of the best possible arrangements of materials for teaching and learning;
   (c) providing available facilities, services, and equipment necessary for the selection, utilization, and management of learning resources; and
   (d) providing facilities for and assistance in the production of instructional materials, displays, and demonstrations.

5.
Utilization of the Center

Knowledge is doubling every five to ten years, and the rate is accelerating. Learners need resources if they are to be successful in their pursuit of knowledge. The resources, the environments, and the pedagogy needed for effectiveness are available and should be employed by professional educators.

The pedagogy of education is a highly sensitive process. It requires consistent environmental support. When educators are competent to design, arrange, and manage sophisticated processes, they should, also, be provided the resources to fulfill the charge given them.

The triad of education consists of the teacher who manages learning experiences, the environment which houses and supports the learner, and the media with which the learner interacts. Weakness in any part of the triad results in weakened educational opportunities for the learner.

Learning Styles and the IMC

Characteristics of individuals are complex within any given group of learners. The variations in cultural environment, past experience, physical, mental, and emotional make-up, needs, goals, attitudes, and perceptual skills influence the classroom teacher in the selection of media and environments for learning. Teachers also must consider each student's level of maturity and background of experience in order to judge whether the content of the media is too easy or too difficult and whether the instruction should be in a group or individualized environment.

Our educational system has been dominated for several generations by large-group or whole-class instructional techniques. It has been a "given" assumption that the individual student would learn from these techniques. Most students do learn, but many, particularly those with deficiencies or styles that do not tolerate the large-group mode, learn less than they must to survive in the educational system and eventually in our complicated society. At best, much of group instruction is less effective than it needs to be to provide an optimum education for individual learners.

More and more school systems, therefore, are turning to alternative methods. Techniques include balanced applications of large-group, small-group, self-instruction, and other cost-effective techniques, including the use of the mass media of commercial television, radio, newspapers, and magazines. In all of these alternatives, the school IMC plays a central role in helping to provide environments and media for learning.

The educational system has had to change to meet the individual needs of learners in the system. Instructional media technology has become an essential component, with machines taking over parts of the instructional and management process, thus freeing the talents and energies of teachers for more creative and vital aspects, including the personal development of the student and the design and preparation of the critically needed software to truly individualize instruction. Again, the IMC's environment and media play central roles in this development and utilization by supplying the space, the media, and the professional staff to assist the teacher.

Within this context, individualized instruction is viewed as a vital part of an education system designed to meet the needs of students. To see the role that the IMC plays in individualized instruction, a clear definition and the characteristics found among the four major types of such programs must be presented.

Individualized instruction entails learner experiences, leading to behavior changes, that are specifically designed and planned for individual students. These experiences are planned after a careful diagnosis of student needs and interests, involving interviews, written and oral examinations, and interest profiles. Once student needs and interests are established, learning experiences are largely self-directed, self-administered, and self-scheduled, with the teacher acting as the resource person to assist the learner as needed.

The four types of individualized instruction programs, based on who determines what the objectives should be and the methods, materials, and equipment to be used, are identified as: (1) individually prescribed, (2) self-directed, (3) personalized, and (4) independent study. A brief description of each of these will define the central role to be played by the IMC in supplying the support environment, media, and professional staff to implement individualized programs.

In an individually prescribed program, the teacher establishes common learning objectives. All children are required to achieve proficiency in reading, spelling, mathematics, etc., and to go through a specified series of materials and exercises needed to attain the desired levels of performance. Individualization is accomplished in that the student does the work at his or her own pace, and the student helps set his or her time sequences. The behavioral objectives for each lesson, segment, or package are clearly specified, and the instructional materials to be utilized in the study are based on careful diagnosis of the individual pupil and his or her learning needs.

In self-directed programs, the teacher sets the objectives but gives the learner degrees of latitude in determining how the objectives will be accomplished. The teacher provides varying degrees of guidance, but the individual student is left largely to his or her own resources in selecting the materials to be used and in seeking assistance and guidance when needed. With this program, the teacher places high value on individual learning styles and on individual differences in approaching solutions to learning problems.

With a personalized program, the student chooses his or her own objectives from a sizeable list of possible objectives. He or she selects the objectives that appeal to personal desires, interests, and needs. Once these objectives are selected, the student follows a prescribed program with specified instructional materials and methods. Once a decision regarding areas of study has been made, the student enters into a contract incorporating (1) specific objectives, (2) instructional materials and resources, and (3) instructional procedures. The student fulfills the contract by completing a prescribed test or other evaluation procedure.

The independent study program provides the most complete degree of freedom in that the students select their own objectives, instructional materials, and methods of study. This type of individualized program is generally available to and utilized by advanced, gifted, and above-average students. The professional staff plays a critical role in helping to guide students to sources of knowledge in both print and non-print formats.

In most schools, the exclusive utilization of one or more of the four types of individualized instruction is not the whole system of instruction. Most schools will utilize a balanced program, which encompasses large-group, small-group, and individualized methods of instruction, to achieve the educational objectives of the system.

Environments and Services Offered in the IMC

The back-up support to the curriculum is offered, in most schools, through an instructional materials center that offers a unified collection of both print and non-print instructional materials, the machines needed to utilize the instructional materials, and specialized environments that complement the classroom by providing additional medium-sized group, small-group, and individualized study environments. A discussion of the services offered in the IMC will serve to detail for classroom teachers the types and extent of back-up support to the curriculum they can expect and should receive from a fully functioning IMC, manned by a professional staff.

Circulation

A major service provided by an IMC is the circulation of instructional materials and equipment. This includes checking in and out printed matter, such as books, pamphlets, and magazines, to individual students and teachers for a specialized period of time and collections of books and reference materials on particular subjects to serve as classroom learning centers. Non-print materials are also circulated to teachers and students. These instructional materials are available on a short-term or long-term basis. The equipment needed for non-print materials is available, and teachers have the option of utilizing the equipment themselves or of having students within the class trained as student projectionists by the media staff. In many schools, a student projectionist service is offered.

One important circulation service, especially in large junior and senior high schools, is the circulation of instructional materials via closed-circuit television. Many schools have been wired with cables which permit the pick-up of programs in the instructional materials center as well as in selected remote areas and the feeding of this signal to television sets in the individual classrooms.

Reference

Another important service provided within the instructional materials center and critical to all curricular endeavors is the provision for reference materials, such as books, periodicals, newspapers, monographs, encyclopedias, indexes, atlases, gazetteers, maps, globes, etc., needed for individualized study by students. In addition, facilities must be provided for individual viewing of projected materials and listening to audio recordings. These reference services are provided in student study carrels; tables that provide areas equipped with tape recorders and record players to which earphones have been attached; and quiet study areas and rooms where students can perform independent study. Some instructional materials centers provide listening facilities utilizing a dial-access system. With this system, the student does not handle the tape or disc recordings, but goes to a study carrel equipped with a set of earphones. Using a telephone-like dial, he or she selects the appropriate program. The audio information, originating from a master console in the IMC, is supplied via cable to the study carrel. These remote stations can be located throughout the school building, thereby providing a mini-environment that supplements the classroom or IMC study spaces. Some instructional materials centers also provide small viewing and listening rooms which can be utilized by groups of students to view sound super 8mm or 16mm motion picture films.

Production

The third major function of an individual school IMC is to provide an environment and the staff necessary to assist teachers and/or students in the production of instructional materials that cannot be purchased through commercial sources, or materials that need to be adapted or modified to meet the specific needs of the school curriculum. This environment must provide space to accomplish the following functions:

1. Basic facilities and equipment are needed for mounting and preserving flat materials, such as pictures, maps, charts,

Utilization of the Center

posters, graphs, illustrations, etc. This area needs to have dry-mount presses, laminating machines (both hot and cold), rubber-cement dispensers, wet-mounting boards, paste, paper cutters, etc. The area also requires hot and cold running water and a large sink.

2. Facilities should be provided for the preparation and production of overhead transparencies, including cardboard mounts and clear and frosted acetate sheets, as well as thermal (infrared), diazo, dry-photo, and wet-photo transparency copying materials and machines. This area must have access to hot and cold running water and a large sink.

3. Facilities for lettering of instructional materials of all kinds must be provided, such as a drawing table and various types of devices, including pen and ink, rubber stamps, stencils, cut-out letters, dry transfer letters, paste-up letter sets, and such mechanical lettering devices as Wrico, LeRoy, Embosograf, and Leteron.

4. Facilities and materials for coloring instructional materials are an integral part of the IMC. Coloring media for posters and charts and for overhead transparencies are especially needed. Water colors, poster paints, pastels, crayons, colored pencils, colored inks—both for paper and plastic sheets—felt-tipped pens, colored adhesive acetate sheets, and other graphics materials are essential to provide the wide variety of items necessary to meet the needs of teachers and students.

5. A still picture, chart, poster, map, and illustration enlarging and reduction capability should be provided in the IMC. Teachers and students should have access to an opaque projector, grid papers, t-squares, rulers, tables, counter space, and an area that can be darkened.

6. Some type of duplicating facility should be provided for teachers and, on a limited basis, for students. These services could include a spirit duplicator, a mimeograph machine, and a multilith or offset press. Usually the

availability of the spirit duplicator and a mimeograph machine are sufficient for all but the very large high school.

7. High-contrast photography and photographic copying facilities are also available in many instructional materials centers. A darkroom, an enlarger, cameras, photographic papers, and the necessary chemicals are needed to provide this service to teachers and students. The ability to copy pictures, maps, charts, posters, etc., onto 35mm slides can add greatly to the creative production of classroom instructional materials.

8. Many teachers have a need for access to a soundproof studio for the production of audiotapes. This facility adds another important dimension to the IMC.

9. The provision for a television production studio adds another area that is provided by many school IMCs. This facility includes studio space for teacher and student productions plus necessary lighting, camera, and recording equipment. With small, portable video recording equipment, the teacher and student can also go out into the community to capture the "real world" for instructional purposes in the classroom.

The environments within the school provide the space necessary for students and teachers to pursue educational endeavors. A careful analysis of activities in which students and teachers engage while using the IMC aids in defining the functions of the IMC and can be summarized as follows.

IMC Activities

1. *Student activities*: (a) seeking information, alone or as members of a committee; (b) reading for enjoyment; (c) viewing motion picture films, both super 8mm and 16mm, and filmstrips and slides; (d) studying with teaching machines, teaching programs, and individual-study modules and packages; (e) learning to use card catalogs, book catalogs, indexes, bibliographies, and reference books; (f) reading

current magazines and newspapers; (g) finding answers to questions posed in study materials, arising from the teaching process or from an individual's own curiosity and desire to explore new avenues of learning; (h) locating and recording data for written reports, book reports, debates, oral reports, term papers, examinations, and research assignments; and (i) communicating with other students in small-group or single-person situations.

2. *Teacher activities*: (a) securing relevant instructional materials and equipment for use in instruction—materials appropriate for general and large-group presentations in the classroom; (b) instructional materials suitable for students working in small groups; (c) instructional materials appropriate for use by students on an individualized-study basis; (d) previewing of all kinds of instructional materials; (e) conferring with the IMC staff on the purchase or rental of instructional materials and equipment; (f) utilizing media production facilities for creation of new or modification of existing instructional materials; (g) consulting with the media staff on administrative procedures in handling special materials, such as government documents, microforms, sample printed materials, and sponsored materials; (h) utilizing inservice programs on equipment operation, selection and utilization of media, and media evaluation as presented by the professional media staff.

Media Offered in the IMC

To function effectively and fulfill the defined role as an enterprise that provides back-up support to the curriculum, the instructional materials center must provide a rich collection of instructional materials and equipment that respond to the individual needs of students and teachers. The basic day-to-day media needed for teaching and learning should include at least the following items. The suggestions for numbers and amounts are based on a student population of 1,000 with a teacher-to-pupil ratio of 28 to 1.

Instructional Materials

Item	Number—AT LEAST
1. Books	11 to 15 books per student
2. Magazines (including adult periodicals for teachers)	Elementary—20 titles Secondary—35 titles
3. Newspapers	Elementary—2 metropolitan and 2 local Secondary—4 metropolitan and 5 local
4. Reference Books	Appropriate to the curriculum; at least 4 different encyclopedias and 2 different indexes
5. Filmstrips, sound and silent	500 or 3 per student, whichever is greater
6. Visual materials: motion picture films—16mm, super 8mm; videotapes	500 or 3 per student, whichever is greater
7. Audiotapes (reel-to-reel and cassette) and disc recordings	450 or 3 per student, whichever is greater
8. Slides (2" x 2" -35mm, 2¼" x 2¼," 3¼" x 4," etc.)	500—including all sizes
9. Transparencies	350 commercially produced plus a selection of at least 35 "master" books
10. Graphic Materials: charts, posters, art prints, study prints, maps and globes (individual items, not sets)	550 separate items

Utilization of the Center

Item	Number—AT LEAST
11. Kits—containing a variety of individual items, maintained as a total set	35 kits in various subject areas
12. Games and toys	200 separate items
13. Models, mock-ups, sculptured items, art objects	60 separate items
14. Specimens	75 separate items
15. Microforms	As available and needed in the current curriculum
16. Catalogs	In high schools—duplicate of guidance department collection: catalogs of universities, colleges, community schools, and technical colleges
17. Professional collections—books	8 titles per professional
18. Professional collections—magazines	14 titles
19. Professional collections—courses of study and curriculum guides	One copy of each district course of study and curriculum guide
20. Pamphlets, clippings, and ephemeral materials	Amounts appropriate to the needs of the curriculum and to student and teacher interests

The instructional materials center also offers most kinds of equipment needed to view or listen to the instructional materials. The equipment will include at least the following items; the suggested amounts and numbers are based on the same student population and teacher ratio as indicated for the instructional materials.

Equipment

Item	Number—AT LEAST
1. 16mm projectors	1 per 5 teaching stations
2. Super 8mm projectors (cartridge and reel types)	1 per 15 teaching stations
3. 2" x 2" slide projectors (remote controlled)	3 per elementary school 4 per secondary school
4. 2" x 2" slide projector (Manual)	1 per elementary school 2 per secondary school
5. Filmstrip projector (remote controlled and manual)	1 per 4 teaching stations (1 remote controlled, 3 manual)
6. Overhead projector (built into the teacher's desk)	1 per teaching station
7. Opaque projector	4 per elementary school 1 per department in secondary 2 each in the IMC
8. Filmstrip viewer	1 per each 25 elementary students 1 per teaching station in secondary schools
9. 2" x 2" slide viewer	8 per school
10. Television receivers (color preferred)	1 per 2 teaching stations
11. Television recorder/players	1 per 250 students

Utilization of the Center

Item	Number—AT LEAST
12. Micro-projectors	As needed in the high school science departments
13. Record players	K-6—1 per teaching station Secondary—1 per department 1 high quality—auditorium
14. Audiotape players and/or recorders (reel-to-reel)	2 in the IMC 2 in the music department
15. Audiotape players and/or recorders (cassette)	1 per teaching station, including the music department 10 in the IMC
16. Listening station (with 8 or more headsets)	12 per school
17. Projection carts	1 for each portable piece of equipment or items that weigh more than 20 pounds
18. Projection screens (at least 70 x 70 inches, beaded surface preferred)	1 permanently mounted in each classroom and 4 in the IMC Four portable screens in the IMC
19. Radio Receivers	1 per grade level in elementary 1 per department in secondary
20. Copying Machines	1 per IMC plus 1 per 25 teaching stations
21. Duplicating Machines	1 per IMC plus 1 per 25 teaching stations
22. Media Production Equipment: a. Dry-mount press	 2 per school, 1 with 24" platen and 1 with a 30" platen size

Item	Number—AT LEAST
b. Paper cutter	2 per IMC (30" and 36" size) and 1 per each grade level
c. Transparency makers (all located in the IMC)	4 different types per school
d. Camera and related equipment	1 Polaroid, 4-35mm single-lens reflex cameras, 1-35mm copy camera w/built-in strobe (to duplicate 2" x 2" slides and filmstrip frames), 2 copy stands with photoflood lights on portable stands
e. Primary typewriter (large type)	3 per school
f. lettering devices or sets	6 different types per school
23. Microform equipment	4 readers plus 2 reader/printers per school
24. Microcomputers	As needed to meet demands of the current curriculum
25. Videodisc systems	As needed to meet demands of the current curriculum
26. Closed-circuit television	Provisions for receiving a signal at each teaching station in the school; the studio in the IMC
27. Portable PA units and lecterns	3 per school

The staff of the instructional materials center will be responsible for securing and distributing easily installed and frequently needed replacement parts and accessories for equipment. These items will include the following:

Utilization of the Center

  (1) projector belts, take-up reels, sound exciter lamps, projection lamps, splicers, and splicing tape or tabs;
  (2) tape recorder reels, splicers, and splicing tape;
  (3) camera filters, copying lenses, and cover glass(es); and
  (4) microphone stands, special microphones, patching cables, and mixer units.

As has been detailed in the preceding sections, the individual school IMC provides an environment that can supplement classroom spaces for instructional endeavors. The IMC maintains a rich variety of instructional materials to support and enrich the curriculum of the school. The IMC has a professional staff to assist both teachers and students in the educational process.

The Media Professionals

A detailed discussion of the responsibilities of the media professional and technical staff will show how the total services provided can be utilized to further the educational objectives of the school system.

With fully integrated educational media services, the pattern of staff organization and responsibilities will result in assignments that provide services to teachers as follows.

A Media Specialist will work with teachers by:

1. Assisting in the selection and planning of educational experiences for students.

2. Keeping teachers informed as to the latest instructional materials and media equipment available.

3. Participating as a member of curriculum committees, study groups, seminars, and panels at various grade levels, subject areas, and/or department levels.

4. Providing inservice programs in the proper selection and utilization of instructional materials.

5. Providing interested teachers with information about the instructional technology field gleaned from reading the literature available in this subject specialty.

6. Participating as a member of textbook selection committees, applying expertise in textbook format, quality and variety of illustrations, etc.

7. Determining and applying suitable criteria for the evaluation of instructional materials and media equipment.

8. Assisting in the application, analysis, and evaluation of research projects conducted by teachers.

Media Technicians, under the direction of the Media Specialist, will provide the following services to teachers:

1. Produce overhead transparencies, charts, graphs, dioramas, maps, and similar materials.

2. Assist where needed in arranging classroom displays, exhibits, and bulletin boards.

3. Assist in designing and illustrating promotional items and publications for the school, a grade, a department, or a subject area.

4. Assist in the preparation of props, graphic materials, costumes, etc., for use with television productions in the school.

5. Assist in the "shooting" of television programs, including camera-work, editing, studio arrangements, lighting, etc.

6. Provide bibliographic searches and assistance in locating instructional materials—and all aspects of information and materials-processing needed to supplement the curriculum.

7. Photograph and develop all kinds of still pictures for instructional purposes, publicity, promotion, and record-keeping, including photographing items for slides, filmstrips, and resources files.

8. Do minor repairs on all equipment used by teachers and students, including motion and still projectors, television receivers and recorders, remote-access equipment, audio machines, computer components, programmed instruction equipment, etc.

9. Repair instructional materials used by teachers and students, including motion picture films, filmstrips, books,

audiotapes and cassettes, videotapes and cassettes/cartridges, etc.

10. Assist teachers and students in mounting and preserving flat pictures, maps, graphs, charts, posters, diagrams, etc., needed for instructional purposes.

11. Assist in the operation of tape recorders, proper microphone selection and placement, and use of mixers and editing equipment needed to produce audiotapes for classroom or individualized instructional purposes as requested by teachers and students.

12. Secure and schedule the use of instructional materials and equipment requested by teachers for both classroom and individualized instruction purposes.

13. Prepare and distribute to teachers, for their ordering and/or information purposes, catalogs, brochures, newsletters, and announcements of instructional materials, equipment, and services available in the IMC.

14. Assist in the maintenance of the physical environment of the IMC in a manner that encourages and facilitates its use, including the proper shelving of print materials (books, pamphlets, magazines, newspapers, etc.), instructional materials (pictures, filmstrips, maps, charts, slides, overhead transparencies, etc.), and the arrangement of study areas.

Utilizing the IMC

The primary purpose for providing the environment, the instructional materials, and the trained professional and technical media staff is to facilitate learning. Utilization is the engagement of resources and learners to achieve desired and needed objectives. Media professionals assist teachers and learners as they consult, interact, and react with the users of the media in the environment of the IMC and the classroom.

Utilization deals with the interaction between the learner and the medium available within a specific environment. Utilization is the interaction, reaction, or engagement of the learner with ideas and with the important medium of communication within an environment that permits and encourages learning; it is during utilization that change in behavior (or learning) is likely to occur.

The effective utilization of instructional materials requires that teachers use a *systematic* approach to the development of learning sequences. The total system must encompass:
- the learners,
- the objectives and content of the lesson(s),
- the methods to be utilized in the instruction,
- the instructional materials to be utilized, including consideration of unique strengths and weaknesses,
- the facilities or environment,
- the supporting equipment, and
- the student and teacher evaluation of the results, in changed behavior and attitudes.

The media professionals, utilizing the environment and instructional materials of the IMC, assist teachers and students to interact with media to achieve desired learning outcomes. There are five major phases in implementing a total system of instruction that must be considered in order to assure that outcomes will be as rewarding as possible. The five phases are identified as: (1) introduction, (2) development, (3) organization, (4) summarizing, and (5) evaluation.

The *introduction phase* is intended to be motivational and exploratory in nature. Students during this phase determine whether the course of study will be interesting and challenging to them. Instructional materials utilized can range from an overview sound motion picture, a filmstrip, a set of 2 x 2-inch slides, an overhead transparency set, etc. Carefully constructed bulletin boards, exhibits, and displays will also help to motivate and challenge students. This introduction is generally confined to the individual classroom environment, with supplementary instructional materials and equipment borrowed from the IMC.

Utilization of the Center

Whenever instructional materials are utilized in the classroom, the successful teacher must consider the following:

1. *Prepare Yourself.* Preview and evaluate the instructional materials so that they can be effectively integrated in the unit of study, both as introductory and as follow-up study (if applicable).
2. *Prepare the Presentation.* Determine how the media will be most effectively presented. If the format of the material is projected and/or audio, the following *presentation factors* should be considered:
   a. Show all the way through?
   b. Show only excerpts or specific segments/frames?
   c. Show with recorded narration?
   d. Show without recorded narration?
   e. Pause at specified points for either added verbal comment or critical study of projected information?
   f. Repeat segments?
   g. Combine two or more media?
3. *Prepare the Student.* Make sure your students know *what* they are going to see, *why* they are going to see it, and *what* they are *expected* to learn from the presentation.
4. *Prepare Follow-up Activities.* Plan in advance what you and the students are going to do after the presentation. Will there be a review of content? What kind of evaluation? What kind and how many projects? What further study will be required?

The *development phase* of the study sequence involves the location and learning of the required information by the students. Because the problem under study may be segmented to facilitate all available alternative options of methodology for acquiring the knowledge—study by individuals, groups, or the entire class—the instructional materials center environment, the instructional materials, and the staff will be heavily involved in this phase.

Instructional materials used are different from those in the introduction phase. The materials are intended to supply the needed information to answer or facilitate the objectives and outcomes of the unit of study. These materials could include all the resources of the IMC. Study centers might be set up in the classroom, the IMC, or in other appropriate spaces in the school to provide mini-environments containing pertinent information to support the students' quest for knowledge.

Even during this phase, there may be some materials that are selected to be used by the entire class—materials needed to provide information important to all students, or detailed relationships of various segments of the entire project. The materials, as indicated in the introduction phase, must be carefully selected and presented.

The *organization phase* of the sequence is intended to be the time for the "pulling-together" of the results of the research and study activities of the students. During this stage, the production capabilities of the IMC are heavily utilized. The most useful materials are those which students make or use to assist in summarizing their findings. Mounted pictures, slide or still-picture materials, charts, posters, graphs, maps, models, mock-ups, duplicated materials, audio and video recording, etc., are materials that students might make to assist in their summarizations. Dramatizations, debates, reports, panel discussions, role-playing situations, use of resource speakers, etc., are typical of activities that may be planned and developed during this stage. Student planned and executed display centers, bulletin boards, or exhibits are also a part of this phase. Most of these materials and many of the activities are supplied from or utilized in the school instructional materials center.

The *summarizing phase* usually entails a major presentation for the whole class by individual members, small groups, and the teacher. The students make summary presentations; present and discuss the contents of displays, bulletin boards,

Utilization of the Center

and exhibits; and hand in written reports, papers, scrapbooks, etc. The classroom teacher may reshow a film, filmstrip, set of slides, overhead transparencies, etc., that were used in the introductory phase to provide a review and to "cement" together all facets of the study. Any "loose-ends" are tied together, and the class is ready for the final or fifth phase, that of evaluation.

The *evaluation phase* involves two areas of evaluation—student and teacher. It is important in any system of learning that there be an evaluation process. Students need to be made aware that they are to be held accountable for lesson content and ultimately for changes in behavior—changes that prepare them to live and function as contributing citizens in our complex society. The student evaluation of content can be accomplished using many evaluation techniques, such as:

(a) written test procedures utilizing true/false, multiple-choice, fill-in-the-blank, matching, short-answer, essay, or take-home examinations;

(b) oral discussions, dramatizations, role-playing experiences, sociodramas, and demonstrations;

(c) audiotaped and/or videotaped responses or experiences, such as performing a psychomotor skill;

(d) written reports, term papers, or research papers; and

(e) student-produced instructional materials, i.e., photographic slides, mounted pictures, maps, graphs, etc., and the effectiveness of bulletin boards, displays, and exhibits.

The critical evaluation of students' performance will provide information that teachers can use in assessing the unit as a whole, such as:

(a) suggestions for revising and/or refining parts of the instructional program;

(b) evidence of faults in the instructional plan, content, procedures, or instructional materials utilized;

(c) identification of problems arising from either inadequate or unclear objectives or inadequate or inappropriate evaluation procedures or methods;

(d) indications that students were not ready for instruction;

(e) evidence of the need for review or remedial instruction; and

(f) evidence of too slow or too fast a pace for some learners.

Teachers must also perform self-evaluation, especially on the major whole-class presentations made in the introduction and summarizing phases of the instructional system, considering such elements as the following:

I. DID I CREATE A PHYSICAL CLIMATE FAVORABLE TO THE USE OF THE INSTRUCTIONAL MATERIALS, BY PROVIDING:

...... Adequate darkening—if necessary?

...... Adequate non-glare lighting—if necessary?

...... Suitable ventilation?

...... Comfortable room temperature?

...... Furniture arrangements designed to give maximum advantage to viewing, listening, discussing, interacting, and reacting?

II. WAS THE EQUIPMENT AND/OR INSTRUCTIONAL MATERIALS:

...... Arranged in the most advantageous viewing position?

...... Free of ambient, glaring, or distracting lights and shadows?

...... Properly positioned and elevated with the projected beam of light centered on the screen surface?

...... Properly positioned and elevated so all could see without eye strain or physical discomfort? Was the lettering large enough to be seen by all viewers?

Utilization of the Center

...... Properly set up, instructional materials threaded or inserted correctly, in sharp focus, and sound turned on and adjusted to proper volume and tone?

III. *DID I USE THE INTRODUCTION PERIOD TO:*

...... Discuss the objectives of the presentation with my students?

...... Present vocabulary and review materials necessary to understand the lesson?

...... Develop student interest in the presentation? Were the students properly motivated?

...... Give the students specific points for which to look and listen?

IV. *DURING THE PRESENTATION, DID I:*

...... Set a good example by taking an active interest in the lesson by being enthusiastic and involved in the presentation?

...... Observe the students, keeping alert to reactions indicating a need to change the pace of presentation or reemphasize main points?

...... Keep the presentation flowing smoothly, utilizing all items in the appropriate places that I had outlined in my lesson plan?

V. *DURING THE FOLLOW-UP PERIOD, DID I:*

...... Establish continuity of the lesson with other elements of the unit or areas of study?

...... Give students an opportunity to discuss points of interest, clarify misconceptions, and ask questions?

...... Encourage and provide opportunities for students to engage in independent study and/or activities related to the presentation?

...... Make assignments involving different kinds of study skills?

...... Conduct student evaluations to see if the lesson objectives were achieved?

The teacher self-evaluation, coupled with the student evaluation, provides an avenue for critical assessment of the effectiveness of the teaching-learning process and whether, why, or to what extent the instruction needs revision or refinement.

Summary

The individual school instructional materials center has experienced phenomenal growth in recent years in American education. This has been due largely to the increased concern for providing learning experiences for the individual student—concern occasioned by curricular and administrative changes, societal shifts, and technological advances resulting in new and improved communication forms.

There has been an increased need for rich collections of instructional materials and equipment and related services at both the elementary and secondary school levels so that teachers and students can make first-hand contact with the wealth of knowledge that is accumulating at an ever-quickening pace.

The instructional materials center is at the heart of these concerns and needs. Only through adequate provision for and utilization of all avenues of learning can students be properly prepared to function in the complex world of the twenty-first century.

6.
Design of the Center

The full potential for assisting teachers and students in their curricular endeavors can only be realized if the physical environment of the instructional materials center is carefully planned. Teachers and media specialists must have a hand in any planned renovation or new IMC construction.

Teachers should have an in-depth understanding of what areas constitute the total IMC facility and how each relates to others so that they can assist in the planning. An in-depth understanding of what constitutes the physical environment is critical for teachers if they desire to utilize the full potential of services and personnel offered by the IMC. Only if they know what services and environments should be made available can they truly plan for an individualized instructional program.

Planning and designing an instructional materials center is a complex task, especially if the full potential of instructional media technology is to be realized. Instructional materials and equipment will be useful to both the teacher and the student only when they are effectively coordinated with basic sensory processes and wisely integrated into the total learning environment of the school.

Much more is involved in this planning than simply transplanting national, state, and local guidelines. Many solutions to local needs and problems must be provided before the architect planning the instructional materials center can proceed with his or her work. The media coordinator and the instructional materials center staff, teachers, and administrators need to be involved in all of the school facilities planning and in the writing of educational specifications.

Educational specifications become a vital concern when designing or remodeling an instructional materials center. Educational specifications are clearly separate from architectural specifications. However, the architectural task cannot be started until the educational specifications are formulated and clearly defined. Educational specifications must describe the activities to be housed, the anticipated number and nature of the people involved (staff, faculty, student, administration), the interrelationships of instructional areas with one another and with non-instructional areas, the equipment, furnishings, instructional materials, etc., and special provisions which deal with environmental conditions that affect student development.

The type and scope of the educational program must be described. What is the educational philosophy? What are the characteristics of the school? What is the nature of the curriculum offered? What type of school organization is used? These are but a few of the pertinent questions that must be answered when planning the instructional materials center.

The key role of the media coordinator and the staff of the instructional materials center in the development of the educational specifications and the final architectural plans requires that they be responsible for coordinating all media and communications systems throughout the school, including audio-tutorial laboratories, language laboratories, multimedia instructional installations, auditoriums, public address systems, small study spaces, student study carrel arrangements, etc. The definition of each space required—using

Design of the Center

national, state, and local standards and recommendations—the detailing of built-in equipment, such as clocks, cabinets, shelving, sinks, etc., and the selection and purchase of furnishing and equipment—are also part of this role assignment.

Basic Space

The discussion that follows on the basic and supplemental space requirements and instructional materials center utilization practices is intended to apply to *a single school* and not to a complete school district, centralized media facility. The space requirements are based on the needs of a school with 1,000 students and an instructional materials center having a staff consisting of three professional media coordinators and two paraprofessional assistants—all employed on a full-time basis.

These recommendations can be adjusted to fit the needs of other various sized populations. It must be noted, however, that all of the areas do not increase or decrease proportionately. For example, the basic area "A" (display, circulation, and exhibits) may not need to be doubled for a population of 2,000 students and should not be reduced for a population of only 500 students. Each area will need to be evaluated individually and the space recommendations adjusted according to the educational specifications of the school.

The recommendations for minimum space allocations are based on a synthesis of the recommendations advanced by the American Library Association and the Association for Educational Communications and Technology in the publication *Media Programs: District and School*, by Emanuel T. Prostano and Joyce S. Prostano; in the publication *The School Library Media Center*, by Carlton W.H. Erickson; in the publication *Administering Instructional Media Programs*, by James W. Brown, Kenneth D. Norberg, and Sara K. Srygley; in the literature found in such periodical publications as

Audiovisual Instruction, Educational Technology, School Media Quarterly, School Library Journal, and *American Libraries* (consult the Bibliography for specific issues); and from the author's many years of experience as a consultant in the planning and administration of instructional materials centers.

The instructional materials center should be located in an area of the school where the functions of the center can relate directly to the other instructional areas. Proximity to major academic areas, a location on the ground floor, and easy access to a loading ramp are prime considerations. The instructional materials center should not be located in close proximity to playgrounds, the gymnasium, the music or band room, the wood, auto, or machine shops, or other areas that generate a great deal of noise and thereby make acoustical control prohibitively expensive.

Many architects plan the instructional materials center to be the center of the instructional area, with the teaching stations fanning out from this center (see Figure 1). Other plans call for the placement of the instructional materials center as the center of a "finger" plan, with the teaching stations running horizontally or vertically away from the centrally located instructional materials center (see Figure 2).

The basic spaces that should be incorporated into any instructional materials center consist of eight closely interrelated areas. The supplemental spaces consist of four areas that should be a part of the IMC. These spaces, however, can be added later if funds are not available during the initial construction stage. The areas and recommended space allocation for each are displayed in Table 1.

Basic area A houses the circulation desk, displays, and exhibits areas, copying equipment, charging areas, card catalogs, reference collections, and periodical indexes. This area has the important responsibility of being the "information" center of the IMC, presenting basic information about

Design of the Center 41

Figure 1

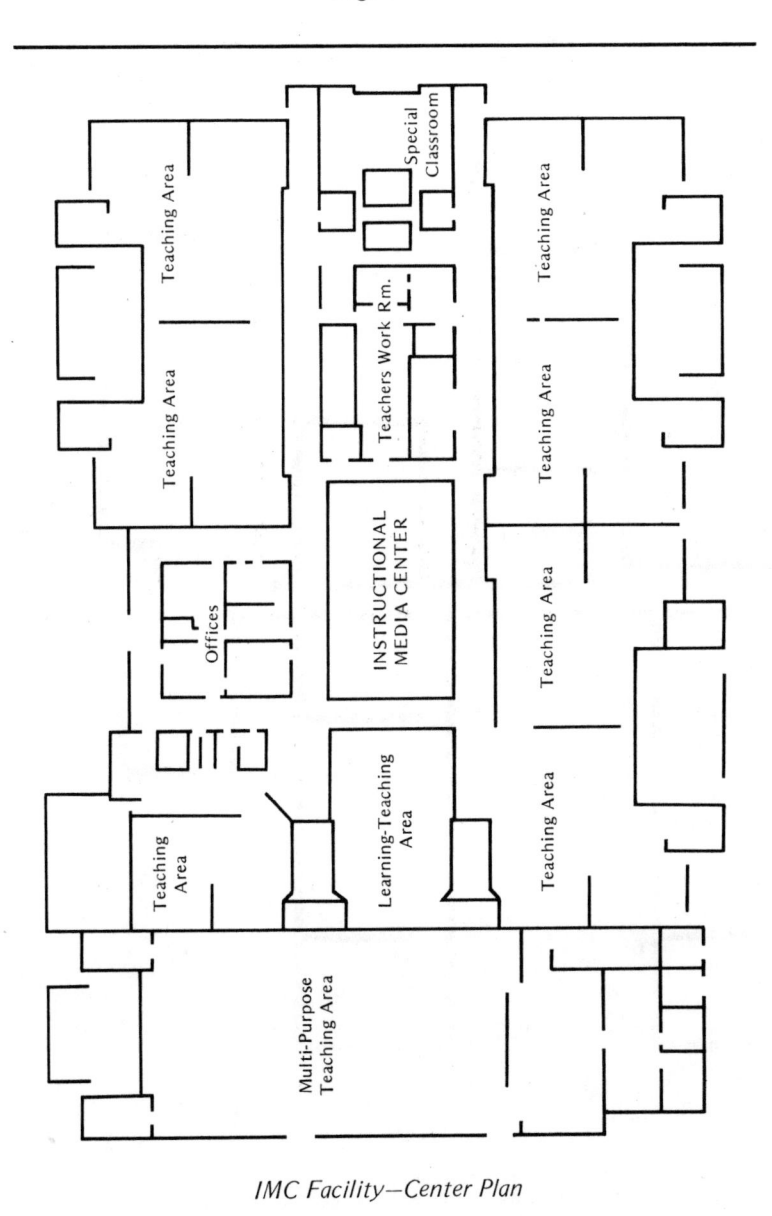

IMC Facility—Center Plan

Figure 2

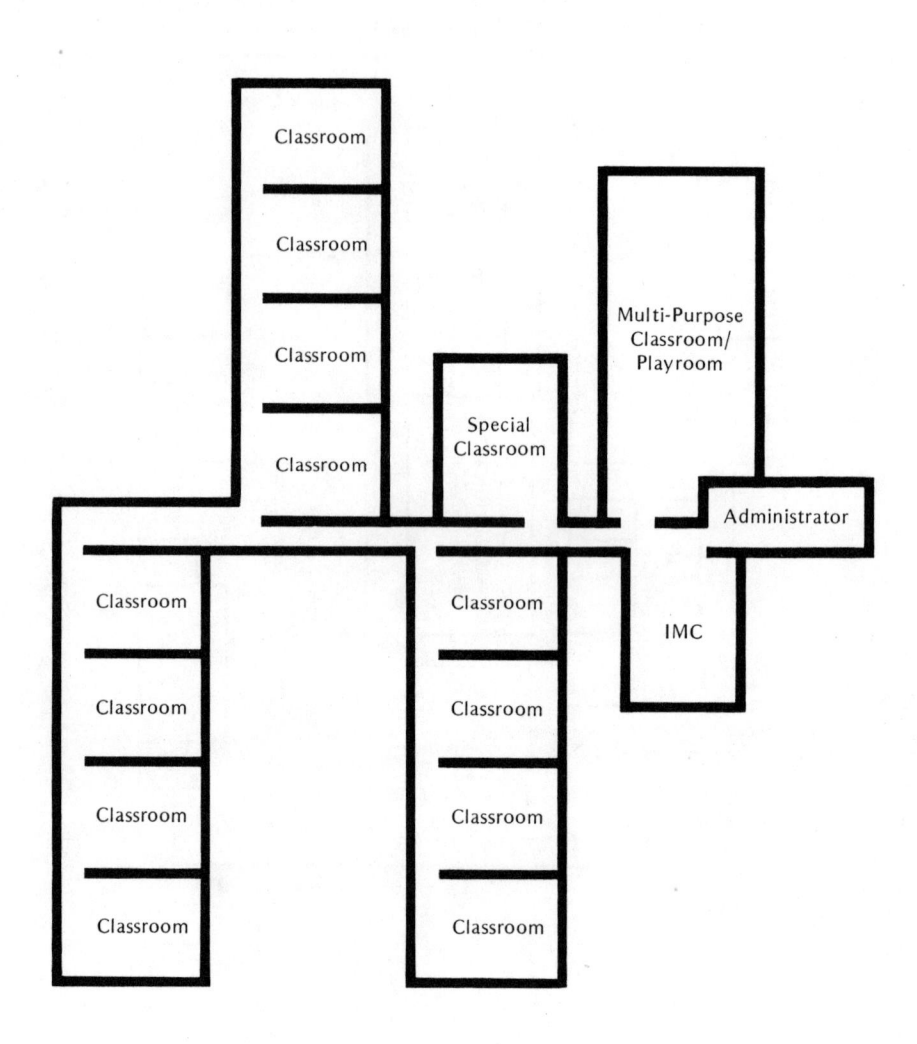

IMC Facility—Finger Plan

Table 1

Area	Minimum suggested space allocation
Basic Space	
A. Display, circulation, exhibits	800 square feet
B. Major reading, study, carrel area	4,500 square feet
C. Small-group viewing and listening, conference room	825 square feet
D. Media production, production supply, storage	920 square feet
E. Equipment storage and distribution area, work space	1,200 square feet
F. Professional collection	550 square feet
G. Administrative offices	540 square feet
H. Stacks, magazines, and newspaper storage	462 square feet
Total	9,797 square feet
Supplemental Space	
1. Entrance lobby, lavatories, coatroom, student lounge	500 square feet

Area	Minimum suggested space allocation
Supplemental Space	
2. Technical services area	650 square feet
3. Television, radio, computerized learning lab	3,000 square feet
4. Group projection-classroom instruction	1,200 square feet
Total	5,350 square feet
Total of Basic and Supplemental	15,147 square feet

Design of the Center

the location and use of all instructional materials, hardware, and production services.

The display and exhibits area should have several bulletin board spaces and at least two display cases, one of which has glass doors that can be locked. This area provides space for announcements of current and coming events, displays of students' written and constructed work, special exhibits that need protection from handling, and bulletin boards of all kinds. Bulletin boards can display personal activities of students, teachers, and administrators of the school (careers, hobbies, sports and games, school life, home life, vacation and travel, etc.), special days and weeks, poetry and literature, unusual happenings, foreign lands and peoples, historical events, etc.

This area may also serve as the main security check-point and the focal point for visual observation of major study areas in the instructional materials center. From this area, the staff will be able to observe students who need assistance, are causing a disturbance, or who are interfering in any way with the smooth operation of the facility.

The functions carried on in this area will include the circulation and distribution of all instructional materials and hardware used anywhere in the school, school district, or community, and scheduling instructional materials and hardware for use at teaching stations, audio-tutorial laboratories, language laboratories, etc.

The card catalog and indexes provide information about what is in the IMC collection. The card catalog should list all print and non-print instructional materials, not just print materials. The indexes should be inclusive enough to list all periodicals available in the IMC and also those available at the district media center.

Figure 3, a schematic drawing, shows an instructional materials center. The shaded area illustrates a possible arrangement within the facility for area A.

Figure 3

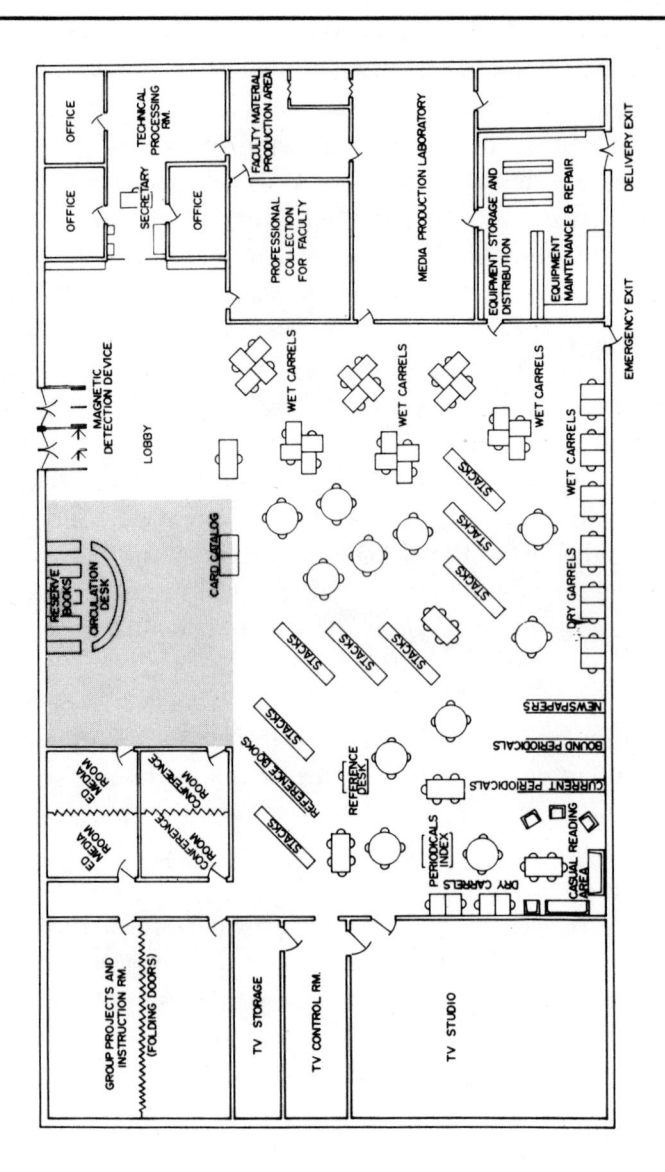

Area A: Display, Circulation, Exhibits

Design of the Center

Basic area B provides space for major reading, study, and student carrels. This area should be large enough to accommodate 15 percent of the total student enrollment (15% of 1,000 = 150 students) at one time with at least 30 square feet of space per student. If the educational objectives detail a high use of media, flexible scheduling, and a great deal of independent study, then the housing of more than 15 percent of the student population will be necessary. The area could require the accommodation of as much as 30 percent of the total student population. If this is necessary, the area available per student will need to be reduced or the total increased above the recommended 4,500 square feet. It is recommended that the space be increased rather than to reduce the available space per student, as the total program may be hampered, in the long run, if the space per student is drastically reduced.

The total square footage recommended for this area need not be available in one large space of the instructional materials center. Media coordinators working in the field find that the total space is better utilized if carefully planned into coordinated reading and study areas rather than one large open space. The shaded area in Figure 4 illustrates some possible arrangements for this total space.

Area B will house the majority of the student study carrels. There should be provisions for a minimum of 20 and a maximum of 48 study carrels for a student population of 1,000 students. A minimum of nine square feet of floor space will be required per single carrel, including chair space. The majority (60% or more) of the student carrels should be wired for electrical power and coaxial cable for television and centralized audio communication. Grouping of student study carrels is preferable over long rows of carrels. Figure 5 illustrates some possible student study carrel arrangements.

Students should also have access to non-electricity-equipped study carrels, as well as to tables and desks that

Figure 4

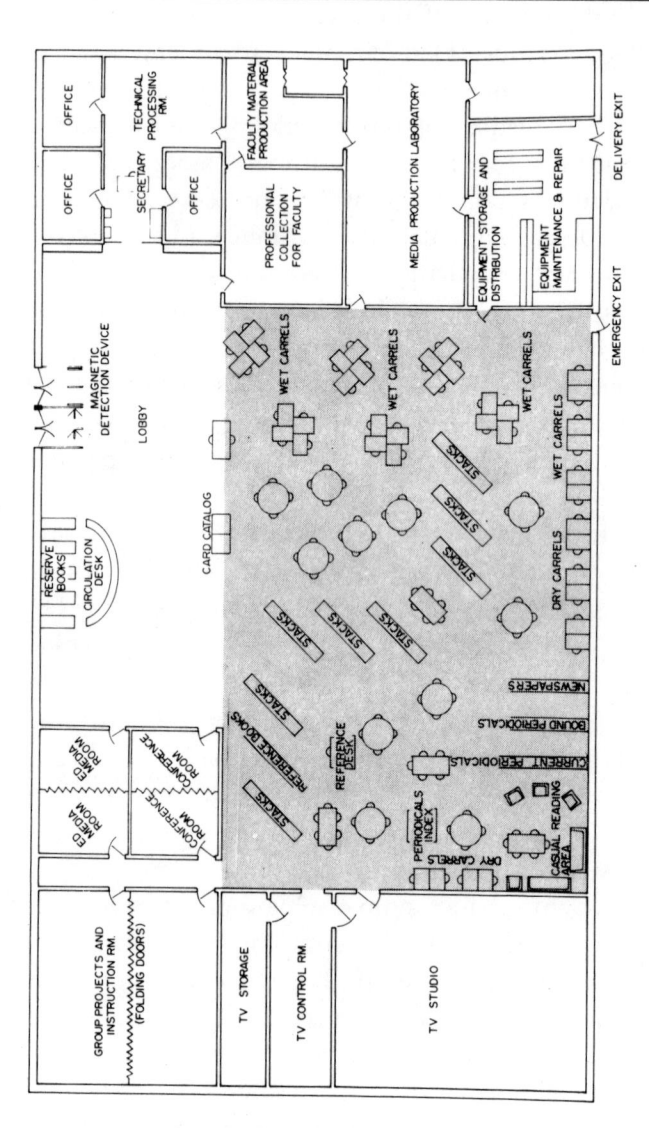

Area B: Reading, Study, Carrels

Design of the Center 49

Figure 5

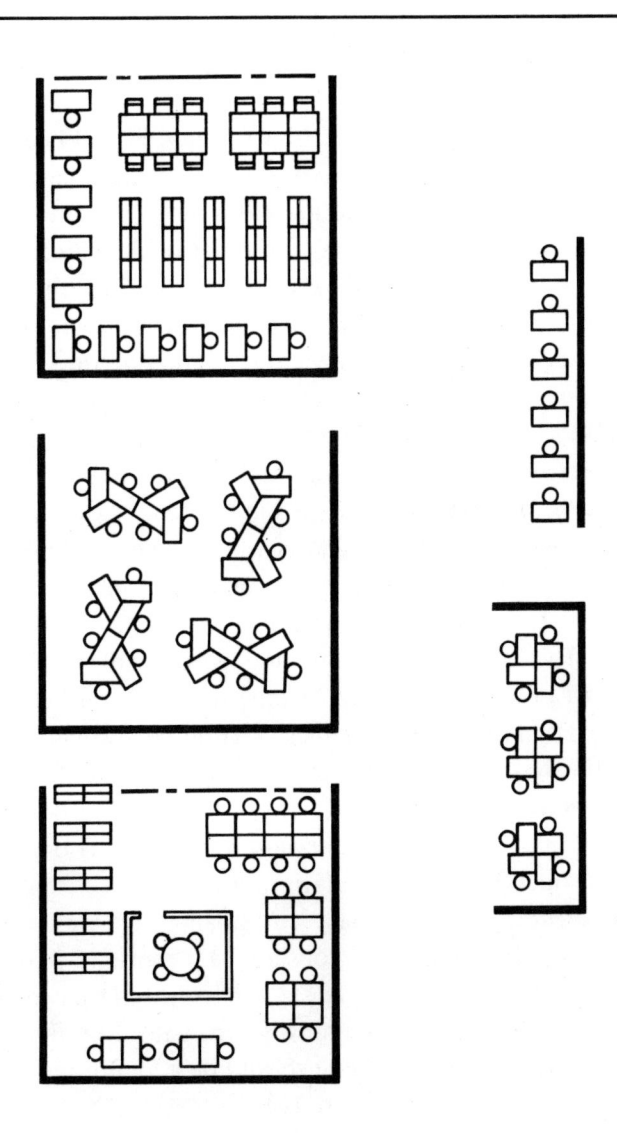

Student Study Carrel Arrangements

provide individual study areas which will not need electrical outlets for machines or video or audio connections to a centralized console. These areas should be quiet, with students not disturbed by groups of people talking or machines running.

Instructional materials in various formats should be housed on shelves or in storage cabinets. These instructional materials will be placed at strategic locations next to student study carrels, individual study tables, and quiet reading areas—within easy reach of the students who desire to utilize them. The reserve area for reference materials may be either an open or closed space and should be near the circulation desk and the card catalog.

It is recommended that the shelving and cabinet space for area B accommodate a minimum of 40 items per student, exclusive of the textbooks utilized in the teaching stations.

Area B will also contain spaces where students can read in a quiet, comfortable sphere. These areas will include a great variety of furniture, from bean-bag chairs to over-stuffed couches. This area could include the "Kiva" concept with the sunken area and the landings leading down as multi-purpose space for reading, playing games, setting-up displays, storytelling, theater-in-the-round, etc.

The reading or quiet areas should be away from noise, but should be open to visual observation by those staff or faculty members supervising the circulation desk.

Basic area C provides space for small-group viewing and listening and for multi-use conference rooms. It is recommended that there be at least one room designed as a small-group viewing and listening room, with a minimum of 225 square feet of space. There should be a minimum of four conference rooms of 150 square feet of space each.

The small-group viewing and listening room must have sufficient electrical outlets to accommodate all kinds of audio and projection equipment. The room should have a

Design of the Center

built-in speaker system that will deliver the sound from the front of the room to the seated ear level of the persons using the room. The room should be equipped with a wall-mounted screen of at least 70 inches by 70 inches. The room may also be equipped with coaxial cable for accommodation of audio and video signals from a centrally located console. The room must be acoustically treated so that the use of audio and video materials will not create a disturbance by interfering with other functions going on within the IMC.

This room can be located near the equipment storage and distribution area (area E) with great advantage. A location near area E will reduce the need for complete acoustical treatment, will make moving audio and video equipment of various kinds into and out of the room easier and more convenient, and will provide a space away from the main reading, study area. This room should be entered without going through the main circulation, study/reading areas.

The small-group viewing and listening room can also be used as a previewing room for the professional media staff, the administration, and the faculty of the school.

The areas that constitute the conference rooms (recommendation: at least two rooms of 150 square feet each per 500 students) must allow for multi-purpose activities, including group discussion and interaction, project and module development, and listening and viewing. It is advisable to cluster these rooms into units of two or more, providing movable partitions which will make the space adaptable for seminar groups, medium-sized discussion groups, medium-sized viewing and listening groups, or a small classroom instruction area. These areas could also be used for temporary display or highlighting of special collections, functions, or events. Many media coordinators use these areas for housing special collections of materials which do not need to be continuously utilized on a day-to-day basis.

The conference rooms also need to be located in a quiet

area of the IMC and should be equipped with electrical and TV inputs and outlets. The areas should have acoustical controls that provide a signal-to-noise ratio of at least ten decibels. The shaded area in Figure 6 shows a suggested placement of these rooms within the IMC.

Basic area D will house two units: the media production area/laboratory and the production supply storage area. The media production laboratory should contain a minimum of 800 square feet of space, and the supply storage area should contain at least 120 square feet of space. If an extensive student production program in graphic materials is carried on in the school, this space will need to be expanded to support these activities. It is recommended that the area be increased by one percent for each additional student who will use the area for production activities, i.e., 800 square feet will provide daily working space for one professional graphic specialist and one paraprofessional graphic artist. Ten students will increase needed space by at least 80 square feet.

The media production laboratory must provide counter space, table space, shelving space, and open space to accommodate such production devices as a dry-mount press, duplicating machines (both spirit and stencil processes), overhead transparency machines (diazo, photocopy, electrostatic, thermal), paper cutter(s), laminating devices, lettering instruments (Wrico, Leroy, rubber stamp, stencil, Embosograph, Leteron, etc.), picture enlarging and reducing machines (opaque projector, Pantograph, etc.), a primer (large type) typewriter, rulers, t-squares, etc.

This area requires temperature and humidity controls, sinks with running (hot and cold) water, a great number of electrical outlets, and ventilation to the outside of the building. The area should have a wall-mounted screen of at least 70 inches by 70 inches in size. Audio production in the area will require a special acoustically treated space, preferably walled off on all four sides.

Design of the Center 53

Figure 6

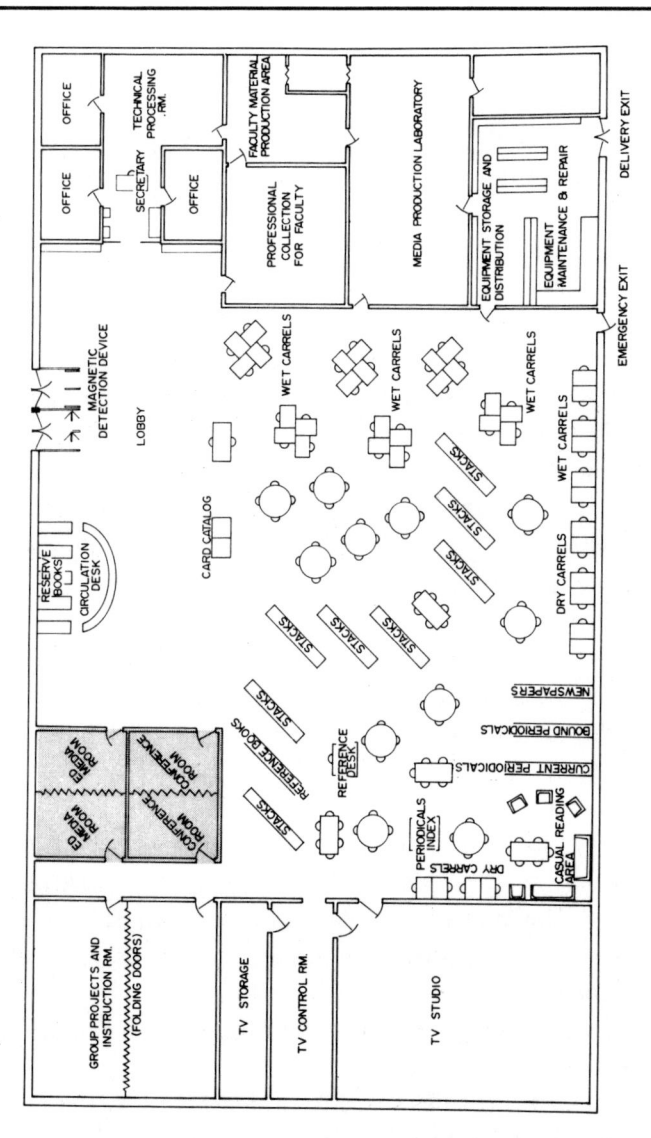

Area C: Conference, Preview/Listening Rooms

A darkroom, containing 150-200 square feet of space, may be included in the media production laboratory. The darkroom will require at least one sink (48 inches long by 24 inches wide), running water (hot and cold with a temperature control valve), electrical outlets, a light lock (light-proof entrance), counter space, light controls on at least three separate circuits, and adequate ventilation to the outside of the building.

The storage area will require shelving of various widths and lengths, cabinets that have full closure doors of various widths, lengths, and depths to accommodate large and small paper products and graphic production supplies, and a refrigerator to store photographic film and paper and diazo overhead transparency film. Figure 7 shows a suggested arrangement of the media production laboratory, including a darkroom and production supply storage area.

Textbooks, magazines, subject-oriented curriculum guides, and other related materials that make up the professional collection for the faculty are housed in *basic area F*. This space is used as a place for the teachers, administration, and other members of the faculty to catch up on their professional reading, or to work and meet to discuss curriculum design and implementation.

This area should be adjacent to the media production laboratory so that teachers might utilize the production capabilities if they desire to prepare some instructional materials. The area should have a lounge atmosphere so that teachers can read, study, or discuss problems in a relaxed environment. This area should have a minimum of 550 square feet of space. Figure 8 shows the possible placement within an IMC facility.

Basic area G provides space for at least three offices for the professional media staff. The space allocations should be such that each office contains at least 150 square feet. One of the three offices might be enlarged to contain an additional 90

Design of the Center 55

Figure 7

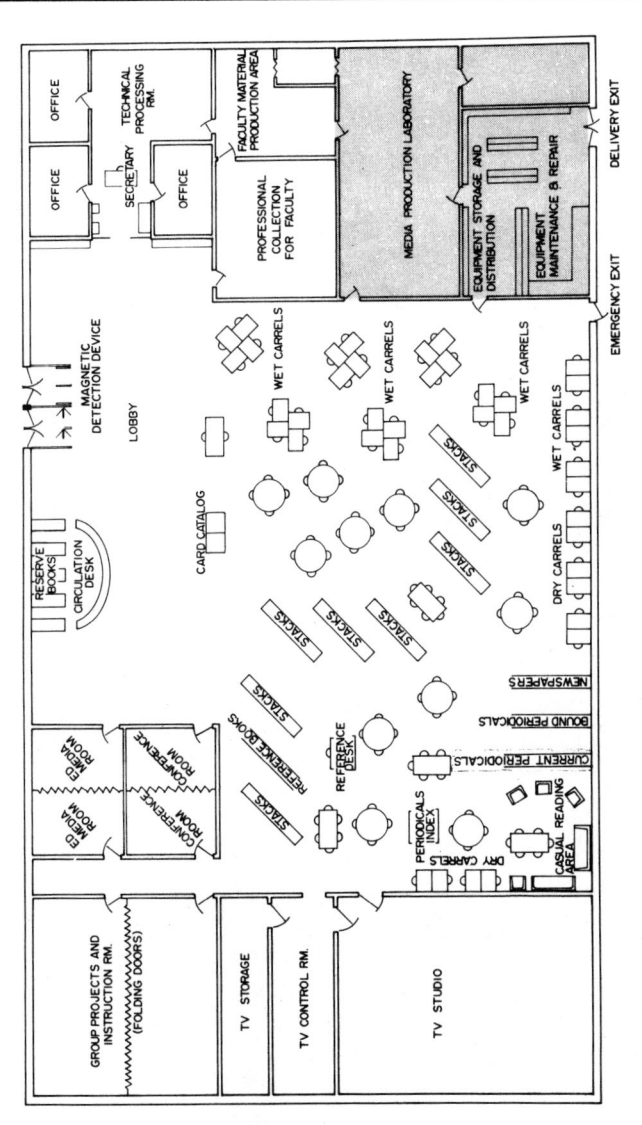

*Areas D & E: Media Production Laboratory and
Darkroom and Storage Area*

Figure 8

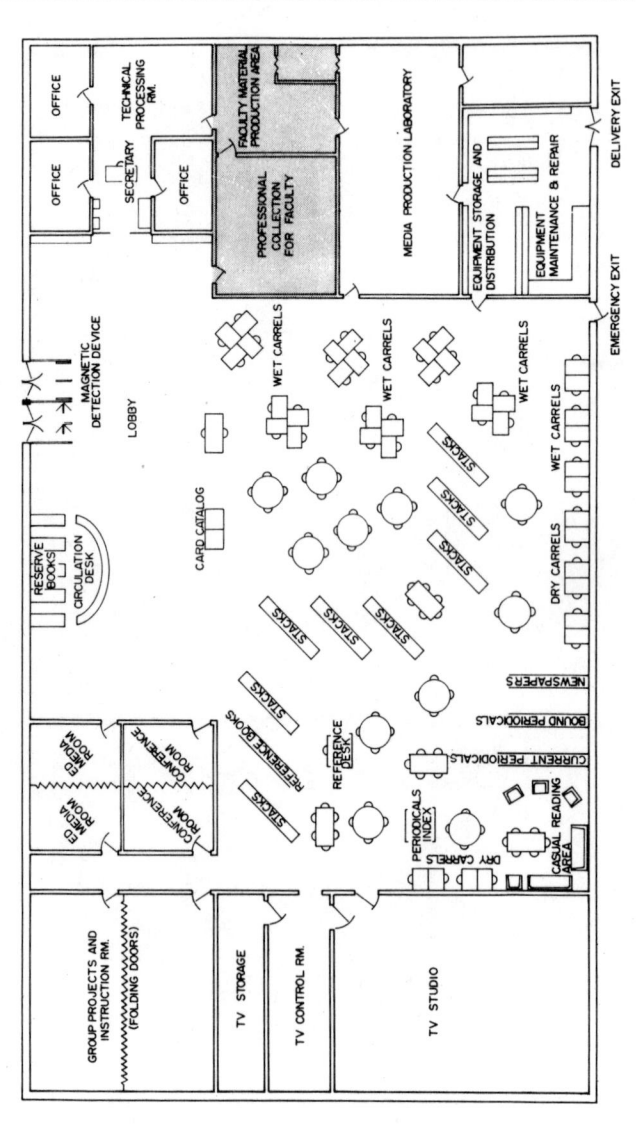

Area F: Professional Collection

Design of the Center 57

square feet, thereby utilizing the total allocation of 540 square feet recommended for this area. The 240 square foot area could serve as the office utilized by the head of the instructional materials center and as a private conference room. This office should be near the professional collection. The other two offices could be located at key places throughout the instructional materials center. These offices provide the media professionals with space for program planning and other work, plus private spaces for study; consultation with students, teachers, and administrators; and a place that can be treated as "their-own." Figure 9 shows a possible placement of these three office spaces.

The last basic space, *area H*, is devoted to book stacks and to magazine and newspaper storage. These combined areas should provide at least 462 square feet of space. The stacks should be located near the reserve areas or where the basic reference materials are housed. In many instructional materials centers, this 462 square feet of space is added to the major reading and study carrel section (area A) to provide flexibility in placement of the stacks.

The magazine and newspaper storage area should be located near the periodical indexes and current periodical materials. It should have space for microform readers and a reader-printer. It is desirable to store three to five years of periodicals in this area for use in class projects. Periodical materials older than five years should be stored on microforms.

Figure 10 offers suggestions for the location of book stacks, magazines, and newspaper storage.

Supplemental Space

The additional spaces needed to support the basic functions of the instructional materials center can be grouped into four types of related service units. These are: (1) entrance lobby, lavatories, coatroom, student lounge; (2)

Figure 9

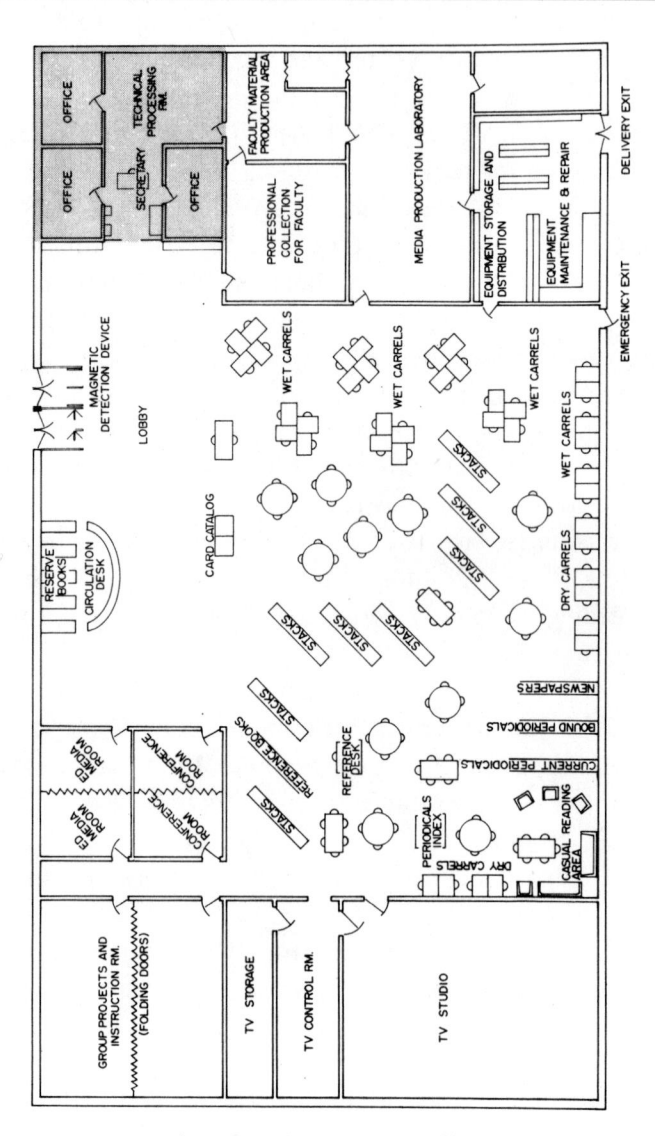

Area G: Administrative Offices

Design of the Center 59

Figure 10

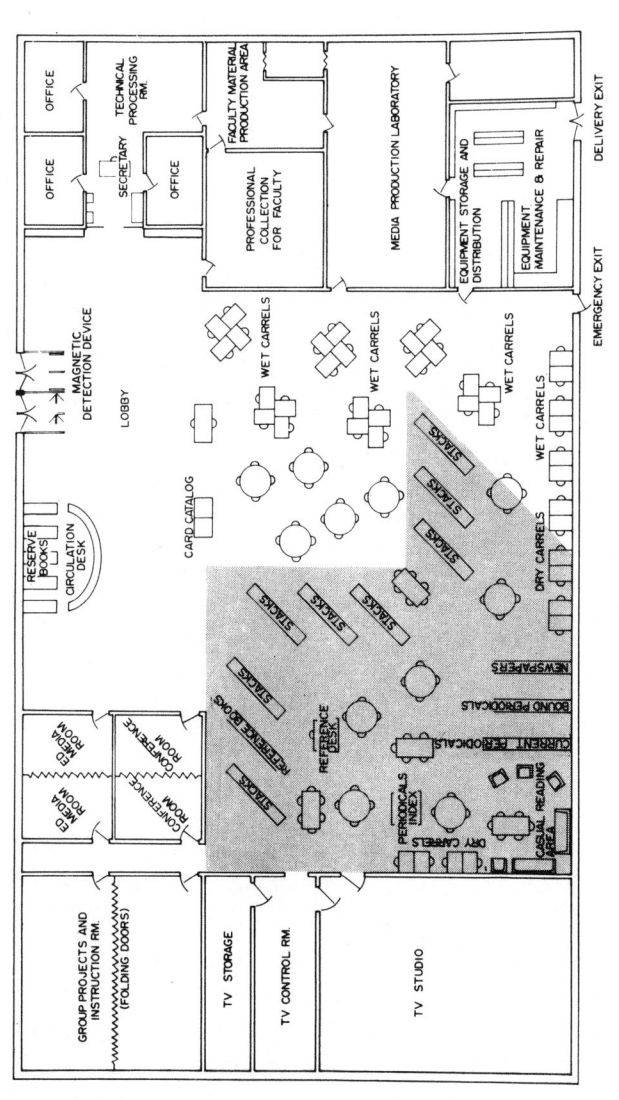

Area H: Stacks, Magazines, and Newspaper Storage

technical services; (3) television studio and storage, radio studio, and computerized learning laboratory; and (4) group projection-classroom instruction area. The need to include these supplementary areas in the IMC will be determined by careful analysis of the educational objectives of the school. If these objectives necessitate an expanded instructional materials program, then the supplemental space will be required to carry out this program. The expanded program will require an additional 5,350 square feet of space.

Supplemental space No. 1 will provide an entrance lobby to the instructional materials center that is large enough to have lavatories, coat racks, and a student lounge. If the IMC is located in the center of the school building, this area may not need to be included in its entirety. The entrance lobby, lavatories, and coat rack area may be located in other parts of the building.

If the instructional materials center is located according to a "finger-plan," then all of the elements of this supplemental unit will have to be included, especially if the IMC is utilized before and after regular school hours. These expanded hours will necessitate an entrance and exit to the IMC that restricts access to the rest of the school plant.

The desirability of having a student lounge is greatly enhanced when the instructional materials center is used during hours when the rest of the school is not operating. The lounge function will provide casual seating, low tables, and attractive lamps and decor. Areas within the lounge could be arranged for small-group discussion, quiet reading, or just relaxing—depending on the furniture arrangement.

Supplemental space No. 2 will provide space for the technical services units needed to support an expanded media program. This room should contain a minimum of 650 square feet of space. The functions carried on in this area will include a centralized section for acquiring and receiving instructional materials and equipment, the necessary process-

Design of the Center

ing services, and space for moving media and equipment out for circulation and distribution. Direct access to a loading dock, an outside entrance, and a wide corridor are required. If the IMC is not located on the ground floor, an elevator to move the media and equipment will be essential.

Supplemental space No. 3 will house three units which are supportive in nature, as the functions are basically production oriented. The three units are (a) television studio, storage, and office; (b) radio studio; and (c) computerized learning laboratory. Together these require a minimum of 3,000 square feet of space. These three units are treated as optional spaces because the extent to which the facilities are needed and utilized in the individual school will be controlled by services and facilities offered at the school district level.

The television studio itself should contain a minimum of 1,600 square feet of space. The ceilings should be at least 15 feet in height, and there should be at least one large door of 14 feet by 12 feet in size. The adjacent television storage space should provide a minimum of 750 square feet, and the television office space should contain 150 square feet. These three combined areas (2,500 square feet) will provide a television facility that can be used as both a production and dissemination unit. The television unit will require extensive sound-proofing, acoustical control, and special lighting capabilities. It must be conveniently located near the media production areas so that television graphics and production sets can be produced.

The size of the computerized learning laboratory will depend on the nature of the computer usage made by the individual school. If an extensive computer program is utilized in the school, the total space needed for this computerized function may exceed 500 square feet of space. This space accommodates computer terminals and storage for CAI materials.

The radio studio should be located near the television

studio so that multi-use can be made of the expensive electronic components required for both areas. The radio studio will have a minimum of 250 square feet of space.

The final supplemental space, No. 4, is perhaps the most important. It provides for specialized classroom instruction, inservice programs, group listening/review, and student projects. This area provides flexible space containing a minimum of 1,200 square feet. This space may serve as a previewing/listening room for evaluation of instructional materials. The classroom will need to be equipped for audio and visual presentations. It will need to have a large (9 feet by 12 feet) wall-mounted screen, wall-mounted loudspeakers, adequate electrical outlets, and acoustical controls.

Figure 11 displays a suggestion for the placement of the supplementary areas within the context of a total IMC facility plan.

Patron Traffic Flow

Consideration must be given to the problems of designing the instructional materials center so that traffic patterns allow users to go to where they desire in the shortest possible time with the least inconvenience and disturbance to themselves and others. Care must be taken in the placement of the units so that a maximum of control can be provided with a minimum use of IMC staff time.

Patron traffic must be able to move smoothly through the entrance lobby to the other areas. Displays that stop the traffic flow for long periods of study should be discouraged. The circulation area should provide enough space for students to study the card catalog and to secure reference materials and assistance without causing a "bottle-neck" in the traffic flow. From the circulation and reference area, users should be able to move quickly and quietly to the major reading, study, and carrel area. Visual observation and control of the reading, study, and carrel area should be possible from the circulation desk.

Design of the Center 63

Figure 11

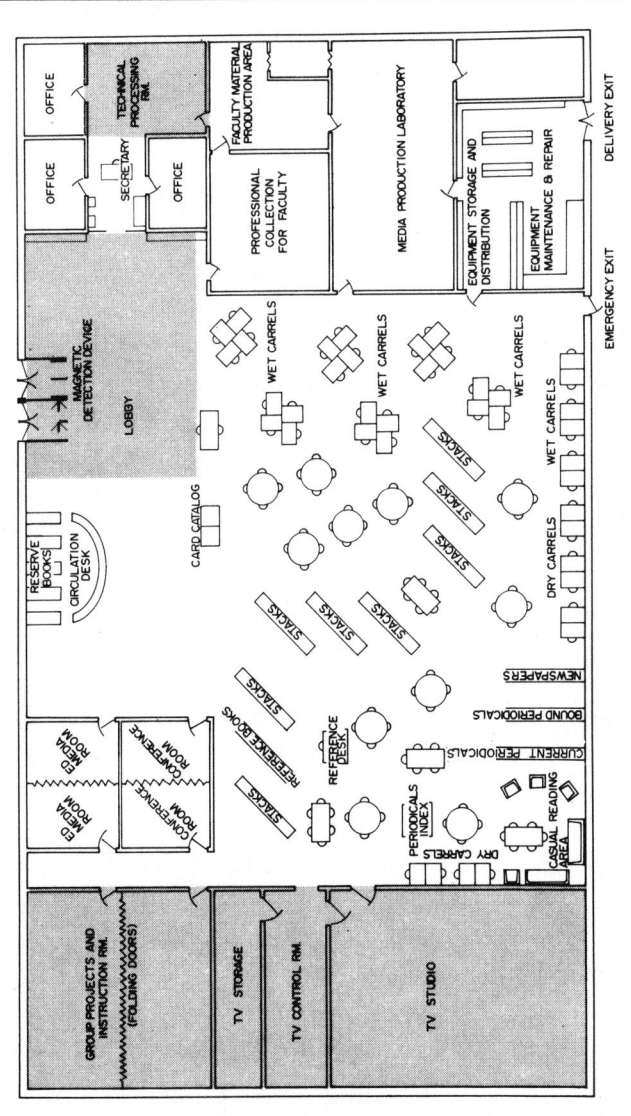

Supplemental Spaces of the IMC

Student use of the small-group viewing and listening rooms should be done with a minimum amount of traffic through the reading, study, and carrel area.

Traffic to the media production section should not be through the major reading, study, and carrel area. Access routes should be from outside corridors, and student traffic flow should be at a bare minimum.

The equipment storage and distribution area should be adjacent to the circulation section, and it should have access routes other than through the reading, study, and carrel area of the IMC. Teachers and students should be able to pick up and return equipment with no interference to others.

The administrative offices can be placed where the professional staff utilizing the office spaces can have visual control of key areas of the IMC. These offices can be placed at those locations throughout the IMC that make it possible for the staff to perform their functions and also to maintain visual surveillance of students using the IMC.

The professional collection should be placed in a low traffic area.

Environmental Control Factors

The learning environment created in the instructional materials center is an important factor in attracting students and teachers into the facility to profitably spend their time in pursuit of knowledge. Students and teachers no longer are drawn to rigid blocks and spaces in a learning environment; rooms which have poor acoustical control and allow harsh sounds to abound; rooms that do not have adequate air circulation and ventilation; and rooms full of uncomfortable, rigid furniture, dull color combinations, and poor lighting. Some general environmental control factors apply to all spaces in the instructional materials center.

Lighting
The optimum illuminated environment for learning results

Design of the Center 65

when an effective coordination of quality, quantity, and direction of lighting is achieved. The reading, study, and carrel area, the small-group viewing and listening areas, the administrative offices, stacks, equipment storage, and distribution sections should all have 30-50 foot candles of illumination. The media production area should have 100 foot candles of illumination. All rooms used as projection facilities should be equipped with dimmer controls.

It is recommended that desks, tables, shelves, cabinets, etc., have a matte finish that affords 30-50% reflectance. The floors should be either wood, tile, or carpet and should also be within this reflectance range.

Most research on visual acuity and comfort suggests that there is little difference between fluorescent and incandescent lights. The selection of which to use in the lighting systems of the IMC should be based on utilization rather than visual factors. It is recommended that incandescent lighting be used when variable intensities and directional controls are needed; use fluorescent lighting when illumination needs exceed 50 foot candles and when long life and low heat gain are required.

Color schemes used within the instructional materials center should be considered quite seriously. Research demonstrates that color, both as a surface treatment and as an illumination factor, has some predictable behavioral influences on learning. It is recommended that rooms to be used for discussion and interaction should be decorated in shades of warm colors (yellow, orange, red), and that those areas planned for quiet reading and study activities be done in shades of cooler colors (green, blue, gray). The "warm" colors seem to stimulate creativity and make most people feel more outgoing and responsive to others. "Cool" colors have a tendency to encourage meditation and deliberate thought processes. It has been suggested that people might do their creative thinking in an orange room and then proceed to a green room to carry out the ideas. However, bold colors, such as bright reds and blues, should be avoided for general wall treatment over large areas, especially if the surfaces are to be used as backgrounds for visual displays and treatments.

Acoustics

The most desirable acoustical treatment for the instructional materials center comes about when a combination of factors—including flooring materials, ceiling treatment, the ventilating, circulation, and heating systems utilized, and the size and configuration of various areas—are considered as a unified whole. Much can be accomplished in sound control by simply arranging the book stacks, desks, tables, equipment, carrels, etc., so that the number of students occupying any one area numbers no more than 25 to 50 students.

Easy audibility depends on the difference between the level of informational sound and the level of background noise—the signal to noise ratio. The minimum acceptable signal-to-noise ratio is ten decibels. A room containing a preponderance of sound-reflecting surfaces will be "louder" than a room containing sound-absorbing materials. A room's reverberation time and effect will have a direct bearing on the intelligibility and quality of the sounds and words heard.

Noise reduction can be accomplished by standard absorption and isolation means. Acoustical tile, draperies, carpeting on floors, and sound absorbing furniture generally will control the harshness of sound within the room. It is highly desirable to have all floor surfaces in the IMC covered with carpeting. Although more expensive initially than tile, carpeting is easier to stand on for long periods of time, is excellent as an absorption material, and is easier to maintain and longer wearing than other floor coverings.

Additional considerations for sound control might include: All plumbing noises should be isolated. Flexible connections must be installed near the pump and air chambers to avoid

Design of the Center

"water hammer noises." Piping should be supported with resilient hangers to avoid annoying radiation of water sounds. Fluorescent light baffles must be acoustically isolated. The ducts feeding air conditioning into rooms should be arranged to eliminate the possibility of sound filtering from one room to another. Air velocity should be kept low enough so that there is no noticeable sound caused by air movement—below 1,500 feet/minute velocity. Selection of sound amplification systems should be made on the basis of the speaker system's efficiency and volume and the reverberation characteristics of the room.

Heating and Cooling

Lighting and acoustical factors in the learning environment are major concerns in the design of the instructional materials center. However, thermal factors are important because they directly affect the comfort with which all aspects of utilization are performed. It should be possible to control conditions thermostatically throughout the entire IMC facility, regardless of weather conditions. What is required is an integrated cooling-heating-air circulation system capable of automatically and accurately adjusting the temperature and air-flow required in various areas of the IMC.

It is recommended that those areas of the instructional materials center that are considered as primarily reading, study, and work sections should be controlled with a room temperature between 68 to 70 degrees Fahrenheit, relative humidity between 30-60 percent, air velocity at 15-25 feet per/minute, and 10-30 cubic feet per/minute of fresh air per person occupying a space.

For equipment storage and operation areas, there must be special considerations. If the instructional materials center has a computer facility, the temperature recommendations of the specific computer vendors should be followed.

The 16mm, 8mm, audio- and videotape, filmstrips, and

slide storage areas must be maintained at 50-68 degrees Fahrenheit, with the relative humidity at 50 percent. If the relative humidity falls below 35 percent and rises above 60 percent, emulsion or oxide coating damage will occur, and film and tape will become brittle and may curl, shrink, or lose picture resolution/brilliance.

Summary

Teachers, administrators, students, and the professional IMC staff must be involved in the planning of the instructional materials center. The type and scope of the educational program in the school will need to be considered along with the nature of the students and the community to be served. Basic and supplementary spaces required to provide the environment for learning must be carefully considered. Teachers need to know the various areas and functions that can and should be provided in the IMC so that they can completely and successfully plan for the learning experiences of their students. The environment, the instructional materials and equipment, the teachers, and the students must be precisely integrated in any IMC planning. The nature of each should be considered to insure successful learning experiences for all learners.

7.
Case Studies

Situation: You have been designated as a member of a team of three, consisting of your principal, the district assistant superintendent in charge of instruction, and yourself. Your team has worked with the architect designing an instructional materials center for your school. There has not been complete agreement in size, importance, location, furnishings, or equipment. There is closer, but not unanimous, agreement among the team members, but the architect has ideas of his own. The building committee of the Board of Education, the superintendent, and the president of the PTA have asked you to make an evaluation of the plan submitted by the architect, with which you and the committee do not completely agree, and to resolve the differences between the architect's plan and the committee's ideas for the instructional materials center. What do you think are the possible chronological steps you must take to accomplish the task?

One Possible Solution—you may have others:

1. Resolve the committee disagreements. Develop unanimous agreement within the committee on all phases of the IMC plan.

2. Review the educational objectives for the school and school district with the architect.

3. Based on the review of the educational objectives and the unanimously-agreed-upon plan of the committee, discuss

the differences (one-by-one) between the architect's plan and the committee's requirements for the IMC facility.

4. Resolve the differences through mutual agreement.

Situation: The head of the instructional materials center has observed that students in one corner of the reading and study room are creating distracting noise, even though they are not actually talking to each other. The room has space for about 65 students, and the distracting noise is caused by shuffling of feet, papers, books, and just general "human" noise. What could the media coordinator do to alleviate the problem, short of restricting students in the area?

One Possible Solution—you may have others:

Divide the space up with short book shelves or cases that are low enough to maintain visual control of the area. Arrange the spaces so they will accommodate only 25-35 students at one time.

Situation: The PTA president has come to the instructional materials center to see if the furnishings in the main reading area are meeting the needs of the students using them. The PTA wants to put on a fund-raising program for a needy cause within the school. The president comes to the IMC at a time of low usage and finds the furnishings to be more than adequate for the number of students using the areas. You try to point out that the furnishings are not adequate during "peak-use" times, but you feel that he or she does not totally agree with your assessment of the need; besides, he or she has been to the athletic director, who has indicated a "real" need for new football equipment. How would you tactfully and convincingly demonstrate your needs so you could receive some badly needed additional furnishings?

One Possible Solution—you may have others:

Invite the president on several occasions during "peak-use" time. Let him or her see how crowded the areas are during these periods. If he or she doesn't have time for several visits,

Case Studies

try to schedule at least two, and then prepare some "peak-use" statistics to substantiate the heavy utilization of the areas by students.

8.
Future Trends

The National Defense Education Act of 1958 started the large-scale development of the instructional materials center concept—a facility within the school that provided students with a collection of knowledge presented in more than the book format.

The Elementary and Secondary Education Act of 1965 further strengthened the ability of the schools to provide individualized instructional programs to students in the public schools. The instructional materials center, a facility providing information in all formats, was firmly established throughout the United States with the help of various "titles" contained in this Act.

During the period between 1968 and 1975, the phenomenal growth of instructional materials centers in public schools leveled off and a stable pattern of growth was in evidence. Most new school buildings constructed in the United States during this period contained an IMC, although the supplementary areas (computer, radio, television studios) were not included in the facility in as great a proportion as during the early 1960's.

In November of 1975, a law was passed that will make the future role played by the instructional materials centers even more significant. This law, Public Law 94-142, called The Education for All Handicapped Children Act, is based on the right of all American youngsters, with no exceptions, to an adequate education.

The law gives strong emphasis to the need to educate children in the "least restrictive environment." The method of instruction must provide an *individualized education* designed to meet the unique needs of handicapped children. This means the students often will be "mainstreamed" into the regular classrooms with other students that are not deemed handicapped.

The implementation of this law will have an impact on the functions of the instructional materials center and on the role of the professional staff supplying instructional materials and assisting in the development of individualized instruction. Teachers will need to rely on the services provided in the IMC to develop individualized programs to meet the special needs of handicapped students. The student study carrel concept, small-group study areas, mediated instructional packages, instructional materials in all formats, and a professional staff capable of assisting in the development of individualized instructional methods will take on additional dimensions and greater importance. With handicapped students attending classes with non-handicapped students, teachers will need to have available to them as many alternative instructional strategies as possible to handle the wide range of learning abilities inherent within the students attending their classes. These alternative strategies can be provided within the framework of an expanded instructional materials program housed in a modern IMC.

9.
Suggested Reader Project Activities

1. Train a group of students to be projectionists. With proper training, students can perform all of the projection assignments needed by teachers in the school.

2. Have a student or students design a "projectionist profiency card" to present to the student projectionists upon completion of training to indicate competency in equipment projection techniques.

3. Train students in proper methods of filing books and then have these student helpers do the book filing. They can also be trained in check-out and check-in procedures of instructional materials and can perform these tasks in the IMC.

4. Train students in dry mounting, laminating with plastic, and use of spray acrylic techniques, and then have them perform the still picture preservation for the teachers in the school.

5. Have a group of students design and produce a weekly or monthly bulletin board display in the instructional materials center.

6. Provide an opportunity for a student to conduct a "book talk" for an interest group, either in the school, in another school, or for patrons of the instructional materials center.

7. Have a student or group of students prepare a weekly

Suggested Reader Project Activities 75

or monthly "interest-corner" displaying new books, filmstrips, study prints, equipment, etc.

8. Provide an opportunity for a group of students to make a "mobile" with a central theme marking holidays, birthdays, special occasions, etc. Hang the mobile in a central area of the instructional materials center.

9. Invite students to prepare a "traveling-display," constructed on two large sheets of 12-ply mounting board—hinged in the middle so it will be free-standing and appear as an open book—to encourage student reading of books and announce *Book Week* in November, *Library Week* in April, and *Poetry Week* in October. Let the "traveling-display" circulate throughout the school.

10. Have students prepare a special program, to be presented during PTA Week, that will outline the services provided and available in the instructional materials center. Conclude the presentation to the PTA with a tour of the IMC.

11. Have students join with you as part of the "editorial board" in the preparation of a monthly, quarterly, or weekly "newsletter" originating from the instructional materials center. The "newsletter" can be used to highlight new materials acquisitions, special events, rules, regulations, holidays, coming attractions, etc. The newsletter is an excellent method of communicating with students, teachers, and administrators, and to involve students in creative-writing experiences.

12. Invite students from different art classes in the school to display their work in the instructional materials center. Have the art work nicely framed and displayed with appropriate picture and artist identification place cards.

10.

Glossary of Terms

Audio-tutorial laboratory: a facility that provides study carrels and programs of instruction utilizing magnetically recorded explanations, descriptions, directions, etc., to supplement printed workbooks, projected slides, etc., and used by individuals or small groups of learners as they seek knowledge or develop skills.

Book-talk: an oral presentation about a book, which includes an overview of the plot, a display of the illustrations, and perhaps some background information about the author.

CAI (computer-assisted instruction): a teaching-learning system that has provision for a program in a computer that can be acted upon and responded to by a student at a terminal.

Camera obscura: an optical device which forms a visible image of an external scene inside a darkened box.

Carrels—dry: student study centers that have no equipment provided in them and usually consist of only a semi-private space for independent study.

Carrels—wet: student study centers equipped with power sources and rear-projection screen devices to utilize audio and visual equipment plus individualized study materials in a semi-private space.

Circulation: a service provided in the IMC which includes

Glossary of Terms

check-in and check-out of instructional materials and equipment.

Coaxial cable: a cable for sending telephone, telegraph, and television impulses. It consists of an insulated conductor tube surrounding a central core of conducting material such as copper.

Decibel (abbreviated as db): a relative unit of measure of sound intensity or volume. One decibel is regarded as the smallest change in sound volume detectable by the human ear.

Educational specifications: an in-depth description of the activities carried on in a school, a description of the students served, a statement of school goals, unique environmental conditions, the curriculum offered, and the school organization and management system.

Finger-plan: an architectural design for the school plant which calls for the placement of the IMC in one wing of the building, with the teaching stations running horizontally or vertically away from this centrally located facility.

Foot candle: the unit of illumination produced on or at a surface by spreading one lumen (quantity of light emitted at the light source) uniformly over a one square foot area.

Graphic materials: term used to describe materials that resemble the things for which they stand—realistic, true-to-life, drawn, stamped, or designed materials, such as charts, posters, graphs, overhead transparencies, diagrams, maps, etc.

Handicapped child: a student that has been diagnosed as possessing a condition which makes achievement in learning unusually difficult.

Independent study: an individualized instructional sequence in which students choose their own objectives, their own instructional materials, and their own methods of study.

Individualized instruction: learner experiences that are specifically designed and planned for individual students after careful diagnosis of needs and interests.

Individually prescribed: an individualized instructional sequence with teacher-established learning objectives and fixed sequences of instruction but with student-paced time sequences for the learning of the instructional material.

Instructional materials: all items used for study and for teaching, including books, 16mm and 8mm motion pictures, filmstrips, slides, still pictures, tapes, records, video recordings, real things, models, maps, globes, cartoons, diagrams, etc.

Instructional materials center: abbreviated as IMC—a learning center with the responsibility to systematically collect and acquire all forms of information, catalog and classify them, and house them; and, upon request, make the information available to a learner.

Kiva concept: a sunken space in the IMC that has three to five large step-spaces leading down to a flat area used for multi-media presentations, story hours, etc. The steps and landings and the flat bottom are generally carpeted.

Light-lock: a light-proof entrance to a photographic darkroom. The light-lock permits entrance to the darkroom but does not allow ambient light to enter the interior of the darkroom.

Lumen: the unit of luminous flux (quantity of light emitted at the light source).

Magic lantern: the first slide projector used to project still pictures, using sunlight at first, then oil, gas, and finally electricity as a source of illumination.

Mainstreaming: dealing with handicapped children in the regular school setting.

Media specialist: represents the first level of professional responsibility on the school IMC staff. Includes exper-

Glossary of Terms

tise in the broad range of instructional materials selection, utilization, classification, and evaluation.

Media technician: a specialist who performs technical functions in the IMC, including acquisition, processing, and maintenance of materials and equipment; circulation and dissemination of materials; inventory and records control; information and bibliographic services; production of instructional materials; and repair and adaptation of materials and equipment; under the direction of the media specialist.

Medium-sized group: a study group consisting of at least 15 people and not more than 30.

Mobile: a form of abstract sculpture which aims to depict movement, kinetic rather than static rhythms, as by an arrangement of thin forms, rings, rods, etc. Suspended in mid-air by fine wires, plastic thread, or monofilament fishing line.

Personalized instructional program: an individualized instructional sequence where the students choose their own objectives from a list of many; once selected, students follow a prescribed program of study.

Realia: a general term used to represent any *real* materials employed in classroom instruction. Examples are rocks, flora, shells, preserved animals, artifacts, etc.

Reflectance: the amount of room light which is reflected from a surface to the observer.

Self-directed: an individualized instructional sequence with teacher-established learning objectives but where the learner has degrees of latitude in determining how and with which instructional materials the objectives can be learned/achieved.

Signal-to-noise-ratio: referred to as the difference between the level of informational sound and the level of background noise.

Small group: a study group consisting of 15 people or fewer.

Study carrel module: grouping of individual study carrels to form a cluster of four to eight individual study spaces.

Teaching station: a classroom, a pod, or any other such arrangement in which an educator or educators meet students in the teaching-learning process.

11.
Software Producers

16mm and 8mm motion picture films, filmstrips, slides, tapes, records, kits, maps, charts, posters, books, videotapes, overhead transparencies, games, etc.

Academic Games Associates, Inc.
430 East 33 Street
Baltimore, Md. 21218

Aero Service Corporation
210 East Courtland Street
Philadelphia, Penn. 19120

Allyn and Bacon, Inc.
AV Department
470 Atlantic Avenue
Boston, Mass. 02110

American Library Association
50 E. Huron Street
Chicago, Ill. 60611

Baker and Taylor
50 Kirby Avenue
Somerville, N.J. 08876
or
Gladiola Avenue
Momence, Ill. 60954
or
380 Edison Way
Reno, Nev. 89052

BFA Educational Media
2211 Michigan Avenue
P.O. Box 1795
Santa Monica, Calif. 90406

Bowker, R.R., Company
1180 Avenue of the Americas
New York, N.Y. 10036

Bowmar Publishing Corporation
622 Rodier Drive
Glendale, Calif. 91201

Robert J. Brady Company
Bowie, Md. 20715

Bro-Dart, Inc.
1609 Memorial Avenue
Williamsport, Penn. 17701

Center for Cassette Studies, Inc.
8110 Webb Avenue
North Hollywood, Calif. 91605

Coronet Instructional Media, Inc.
65 East South Water Street
Chicago, Ill. 60601

Creative Audio Visual Materials
Independence Square
Philadelphia, Penn. 19105

Creative Teaching Press, Inc.
5305 Production Drive, Dept. I
Huntington Beach, Calif. 92649

Demco Educational Corporation
2120 Fordem Avenue
Madison, Wisc. 53701

Denoyer-Geppert Company
5235 Ravenwood Avenue
Chicago, Ill. 60640

Doubleday Multimedia
P.O. Box 11607/1371 Reynolds Avenue
Santa Ana, Calif. 92705

Edmund Scientific Company
555 Edscorp Bldg.
Barrington, N.J. 08007

Educational Technology Publications, Inc.
140 Sylvan Avenue
Englewood Cliffs, N.J. 07632

Encyclopaedia Britannica Educational Corporation
425 North Michigan Avenue
Chicago, Ill. 60611

Eye Gate Media
14601 Archer Avenue
Jamaica, N.Y. 11435

Ginn and Company
Statler Bldg.
Boston, Mass. 02117

Great Plains National Instructional Television Library
P.O. Box 80669
Lincoln, Neb. 68501

Hammond and Company, Inc.
515 Valley Street
Maplewood, N.J. 07040

Harper and Row, Publishers, Inc.
10 East 53 Street
New York, N.Y. 10022

Holt, Rinehart, and Winston
383 Madison Avenue
New York, N.Y. 10017

Hubbard Scientific Company
P.O. Box 442
Northbrook, Ill. 60062

Instructo Corporation
Cedar Hollow and Mathews Road
Paoli, Penn. 10301

Libraries, Unlimited
Littleton, Colo. 80120

McGraw-Hill, Inc.
1221 Avenue of the Americas
New York, N.Y. 10020

McIntyre Visual Publications, Inc.
716 Center Street
Lewiston, N.Y. 14092

Milton Bradley Company
74 Park Street
Springfield, Mass. 01101

Modern Learning Aids, Division of Ward's Natural Science
P.O. Box 302
Rochester, N.Y. 14603

National Audiovisual Center
Washington, D.C. 20409

Software Producers

National Center for Audio Tapes
(NCAT)
384 Stadium Bldg.
University of Colorado
Boulder, Colo. 80302

National Geographic Society
School Services Division
16th and M Street, N.W.
Washington, D.C. 20036

NICEM
University of Southern California
University Park
Los Angeles, Calif. 90007

Nystrom, A.J. and Company
3333 Elston Avenue
Chicago, Ill. 60611

Owen, F.A., Publishing Company
Dansville, N.Y. 14437

Pocket Books, Inc.
630 Fifth Avenue
New York, N.Y. 10020

Rand McNally and Company
P.O. Box 7600
Chicago, Ill. 60680

RCA Educational Services
Camden, N.J. 08108

Science Research Associates, Inc.
259 East Erie Street
Chicago, Ill. 60611

Scott, Foresman & Company
1900 E. Lake Avenue
Glenview, Ill. 60025

Seal, Incorporated
Derby, Conn. 06418

Society for Visual Education, Inc.
1345 Diversey Parkway
Chicago, Ill. 60614

Spoken Arts, Inc.
310 North Avenue
New Rochelle, N.Y. 10801

3M Company, Visual Products Division
3M Center
St. Paul, Minn. 55101

Time-Life Multimedia
100 Eisenhower Drive
Paramus, N.J. 07652

Walt Disney Educational Media Company
550 South Buena Vista Street
Burbank, Calif. 91521

Welch Scientific Company
7300 N. Linder Avenue
Skokie, Ill. 60076

Westinghouse Learning Corporation
100 Park Avenue
New York, N.Y. 10017

Wilson, H.W., Company
950 University Avenue
New York, N.Y. 10452

Xerox Corporation
Xerox Square
Rochester, N.Y. 14644

12.
Hardware Producers

Projection tables and stands, mobile storage cabinets, stationary cabinets, stacking cabinets, storage cases, open racks (magazine, book, film), display cases, shelving, bookcases, library furniture, card catalog cabinets, etc.

Accessories Manufacturers, Ltd.
P.O. Box 70
595 St. Remi Street
Montreal, Quebec, Canada

Advance Products Company, Inc.
P.O. Box 2178
1101 East Central
Wichita, Kan. 67214

American Professional Equipment Company
2802 South MacDill Avenue
Tampa, Fla. 33609

Audio-Visual Accessories & Supplies Corporation
196 Holt Street
Hackensack, N.J. 07602

Audio-Visual Specialty Products
6061 West Third Street
Los Angeles, Calif. 90036

Avid Corporation
10 Tripps Lane
East Providence, R.I. 02914

Baia Photo-Optical Corporation
9353 Lee Road
Jackson, Mich. 49201

Bretford Manufacturing, Inc.
9715 Soreng Avenue
Schiller Park, Ill. 60176

Compco Photographic
364 West Erie Street
Chicago, Ill. 60610

Dealers Audio-Visual Supply Corporation
P.O. Box 105
1 Madison Street
East Rutherford, N.J. 07073

Denoyer-Geppert
5235 Ravenswood Avenue
Chicago, Ill. 60640

Hardware Producers

Display Media, Inc.
120 Laura Drive
Addison, Ill. 60101

Educational Developmental Laboratories
Division of McGraw-Hill, Inc.
1221 Avenue of the Americas
New York, N.Y. 10020

Elden Enterprises, Inc.
P.O. Box 3201
Charleston, W. Va. 25332

Ferno Washington, Inc.
Wilmington, OH 45177

Franklin Distributors Corporation
P.O. Box 320
Denville, N.J. 07834

Gruber Products Company
P.O. Box 5556
5254 Jackman Road
Toledo, Oh. 43612

Highsmith Company, Inc.
P.O. Box 25
Highway 106 East
Fort Atkinson, Wisc. 53538

International Visual Products, Inc.
333 Route 46
Gothic Plaza
Fairfield, N.J. 07006

Karl Heitz, Inc.
979 Third Avenue
New York, N.Y. 10022

Leedal, Inc.
2929 South Halsted
Chicago, Ill. 60608

Library Bureau
Division of Mohawk Valley Community Corp.
801 Park Avenue
Herkimer, N.Y. 13350

Library Microfilms and Materials Company
5709 Mesmer Avenue
Culver City, Calif. 90230

Luxor Corporation
P.O. Box 830
104 Lake View Avenue
Waukegan, Ill. 60085

Lyon Metal Products, Inc.
P.O. Box 671
Aurora, Ill. 60507

MPC Educational Systems, Inc.
35 Fulton Street
New Haven, Conn. 06512

Multiplex Display Fixture Company
1555 Larkin Williams Road
Fenton, Miss. 63026

Neumade Products Corporation
P.O. Box 568
720 White Plains Road
Scarsdale, N.Y. 10583

Pioneer Products Corporation
3229 West Pioneer Drive
Irving, Tex. 75061

Plastic Sealing Corporation
1507 North Gardner Street
Hollywood, Calif. 90046

Progress Industries, Inc.
7290 Murdy Circle
Huntinton Beach, Calif. 92647

Research Technology, Inc.
8260 Elmwood Avenue
Skokie, Ill. 60076

Seary Manufacturing Corporation
19 Nebraska Avenue
Endicott, N.Y. 13760

Smith System Manufacturing Company
1405 Silver Lake Road
New Brighton, Minn. 55112

Smith-Victor Corporation
Lake & Colfax Streets
Griffith, Ind. 46319

Squibb-Taylor, Inc.
P.O. Box 20158
10807 Harry Hines Blvd.
Dallas, Tex. 75220

3-S Products Division
Southern School Service, Inc.
Sonoma Road/Highway 215 South
Canton, N.C. 28716

Univex International, Ltd.
3636 South Jason
Englewood, Colo. 80110

Wallach & Associates, Inc.
5701 Euclid Avenue
Cleveland, Oh. 44103

Welt/Safe Lock, Inc.
2400 West Eighth Lane
Hialeah, Fla. 33010

Wilson, W., Corporation
555 West Taft Drive
South Holland, Ill. 60473

Winsted Corporation
8127 Pleasant Avenue South
Minneapolis, Minn. 55420

Yankee Photo Products, Inc.
11295 West Washington Blvd.
Culver City, Calif. 90203

Student Study Carrels and Listening Tables

Advance Products Company, Inc.
P.O. Box 2178
1101 East Central
Wichita, Kan. 67214

Audio Tutorial Systems
Division of Deckmar Design Specialists
P.O. Box 1306
1440 Canal Street
Auburn, Calif. 95603

Audio-Visual Accessories & Supplies Corporation
196 Holt Street
Hackensack, N.J. 07602

Califone International, Inc.
5922 Bowcrost Street
Los Angeles, Calif. 90016

Command Products Company
P.O. Box 1577
Evanston, Ill. 60204

Educational Development Laboratories
Division of McGraw-Hill, Inc.
1221 Avenue of the Americas
New York, N.Y. 10020

Hardware Producers

Educational Technology, Inc.
2224 Hewlett Avenue
Merrick, N.Y. 11566

Fleetwood Furniture Company
Electronics Division
P.O. Box 58
25 East Washington
Zeeland, Miss. 49464

GEL Systems, Inc.
1085 Commonwealth Avenue
Boston, Mass. 02215

Hamilton Electronics Corporation
2003 West Fulton Street
Chicago, Ill. 60612

Howe Furniture Corporation
155 East 56th Street
New York, N.Y. 10022

Huff & Company
P.O. Box 3675
Stanford, Calif. 94035

I/CT-Instructional/Communications Technology, Inc.
10 Stepar Place
Huntington Station, N.Y. 11746

Monroe Industries, Inc.
2955 South Kansas
Wichita, Kan. 67216

MPC Educational Systems, Inc.
35 Fulton Street
New Haven, Conn. 06512

National School Furniture Corporation
2100 Hollywood Blvd.
Hollywood, Fla. 33020

Radio-Matic of America, Inc.
760 Ramsey Avenue
Hillside, N.J. 07205

Rigid-X Manufacturing Division
Southern School Services, Inc.
P.O. Box 867
Canton, N.C. 28716

Synsor Corporation
Bldg. 501
2927 112th Street SW
Paine Field,
Everett, Wash. 98204

The Worden Company
1121 Ionia NW
Grand Rapids, Mich. 49502

13.

Bibliography

Books

American Library Association and Association for Educational Communications and Technology. *Media Program: District and School*, Washington, D.C., 1975, pp. 87-104.

Association for Educational Communications and Technology. *College Learning Resources Program*, Washington, D.C., 1977, pp. 49-70.

Brown, James W., Kenneth D. Norberg, and Sara K. Srygley. *Administering Educational Media*, McGraw-Hill Book Company, New York, New York, 1972, pp. 141-164.

Ellsworth, Ralph E., and Hobart D. Wagener. *The School Library: Facilities for Independent Study in the Secondary School*, Educational Facilities Laboratory, New York, 1963, 143 pages.

Erickson, Carlton W.H. *Administering Instructional Media Programs*, Macmillan Publishing Company, New York, 1969, pp. 175-225.

Green, Alan C. et al. *Educational Facilities with the New Media*, National Education Association, Washington, D.C., 1966, 118 pages.

Hicks, Warren B., and Alma M. Tillin. *Managing Multimedia Libraries*, R.R. Bowker Company, New York, 1977, 269 pages.

Merrill, Irving R., and Harold A. Drub. *Criteria for Planning the College and University Learning Resources Center,* Association for Educational Communications and Technology, Washington, D.C., 1977, 117 pages.

Pearson, Neville P., and Lucius Butler. *Instructional Materials Centers,* Burgess Publishing Company, Minneapolis, Minn., 1969, 249 pages.

Piechowiak, Ann B., and Myra B. Cook. *Complete Guide to the Elementary Learning Center,* Parker Publishing Company, Inc., West Nyack, New York, 1976, 252 pages.

Prostano, Emanuel T., and Joyce S. Prostano. *The School Library Media Center,* Libraries Unlimited, Inc., Littleton, Colorado, 1977, pp. 85-138.

Sleeman, Phillip J., Ted C. Cobun, and D.M. Rockwell. *Instructional Media and Technology,* Longman Inc., New York, 1979, 374 pages.

Utah State Board of Education. *Guidelines for the Development of an Instructional Media System,* Part IV, Salt Lake City, Utah, 1975, pp. 11-23.

Media

Options and Facilities for Learning, sound/filmstrip, color, 20 minutes, Hagerman Individualized Learning Center, Hagerman, Idaho 83332.

Remarkable Schoolhouse, 16mm film, color, 25 minutes, McGraw-Hill Films, 1221 Avenue of the Americas, New York, New York 10020.

To Build a Schoolhouse, 16mm film, color, 27 minutes, Association Films, 241 East 34th Street, New York, New York 10022.

Periodical Literature

Ashcroft, Samuel C. "Learning Resources in Special Education: The Quiet Revolution," *Education and Training of the Mentally Retarded,* Vol. 12, No. 2, April, 1977, pp. 132-136.

Baker, Phillip D. "20 Steps to Success in Renovating Media Centers," *American School and Library*, Vol. 48, No. 6, February, 1976, pp. 98-99 and 102.

Baker, Phillip D. "Exemplary Media Programs," *School Library Journal*, Vol. 23, No. 9, May, 1977, pp. 23-27.

Barber, Raymond W. "The Media Supervisor as Helper," *Drexel Library Quarterly*, Vol. 13, No. 2, April, 1977, pp. 14-23.

Battle, Alice H. "Building Concern Is the Key," *Audiovisual Instruction*, Vol. 17, No. 10, December, 1973, pp. 18-19.

Bennett, Jack A. "Efficient Staffing of the Learning Resource Center," *Audiovisual Instruction*, Vol. 23, No. 4, April, 1978, p. 48.

Brady, R.S. "Pseudopodal High School Can Shrink or Spread Its Learning Center," *Nation's Schools*, Vol. 81, June, 1968, p. 42.

Branscombe, F. "IMC for Old and New Schools," *Audiovisual Instruction*, Vol. 13, June, 1968, p. 605.

Brown, Robert M. "The Learning Center," *AV Communication Review*, Fall, 1968, p. 294.

Bushman, Arlan G. "Barrier Free," *American Libraries*, June, 1977, pp. 81-89.

Butler, Naomi W. "The Planning and Modification of Library Media Center Facilities," *Drexel Library Quarterly*, Vol. 13, No. 2, April, 1977, pp. 62-79.

Cafferella, Edward P. "The Acoustics of Educational Facilities," *Audiovisual Instruction*, Vol. 17, No. 10, December, 1973, pp. 10-11.

Clark, Geraldine. "Echoes of 60's Advocacy in the School Media Center of the 80's," *American Libraries*, Vol. 10, No. 6, June, 1979, pp. 369-372.

Cohen, Aaron, and Elaine Cohen. "Remodeling the Library," *School Library Journal*, Vol. 24, No. 6, February, 1978, pp. 30-33.

Colby, Edmund K. "Elementary School Library Media

Services: How Children View Them," *Catholic Library World*, Vol. 50, No. 4, November, 1978, pp. 158-60.

Connally, Sybil Dee, and Lucy Wollen. "How to Make Something from Nothing: Media Centers in the Urban and Rural Areas Tell How," *American Libraries*, Vol. 8, No. 10, November, 1977, pp. 572-573.

Council of Educational Facility Planners. "What Went Wrong? The IM Center," *American School and University*, Vol. 40, April, 1968, p. 53.

Craig, James F. "What's a Media Gondola?" *Audiovisual Instruction*, Vol. 22, No. 9, November, 1977, pp. 33-40.

Douglas, Harlan L. "Designing Facilities for Learning: An Experiment at Burlington County College," *Audiovisual Instruction*, October, 1970, pp. 57-58.

Ely, Donald P. "The Instructional Technologist: Facilitator of Facilities Planning," *Audiovisual Instruction*, Vol. 18, No. 7, September, 1973, pp. 12-13.

Editorial. "Customizing School Media Centers," *American Libraries*, Vol. 8, January, 1977, pp. 16-17.

Flanagan, John S., and Gary S. Zampano. "Bridging the Planning Gap," *American School and University*, Vol. 51, No. 1, September, 1978, pp. 34-35.

Fleming, Lois D. "Public and School Libraries: Partners in the 'Big' Picture," *School Media Quarterly*, Vol. 7, No. 1, Fall, 1978, pp. 25-30.

Gardner, C. Hugh. "Why Media Budgets Get Cut," *Audiovisual Instruction*, Vol. 23, No. 4, April, 1978, pp. 14-15.

Gorman, Don A. "A Step Beyond the Facilitation of Learning," *Audiovisual Instruction*, Vol. 17, No. 10, December, 1973, pp. 5 and 8.

Greenhill, Leslie P. "The Forum: A Circular Classroom Building," *Audiovisual Instruction*, Vol. 15, No. 10, December, 1970, pp. 72-75.

Haviland, David S. "Designing Multi-Media Rooms for Teaching," *Audiovisual Instruction*, Vol. 15, October, 1970, pp. 78-81.

Hertz, Karl V., and Blanche Jenecek. "Libraries Are Important for Gifted Students," *NASSP Bulletin*, Vol. 62, No. 415, February, 1978, pp. 120-121.

"Instructional Materials Center: Philosophy, Facilities, and Design," *Audiovisual Instruction*, Vol. 12, October, 1967.

Johnson, Harlan R. "Teacher Utilization of Instructional Media Centers in Secondary Schools," *Clearing House*, Vol. 51, No. 3, November, 1977, pp. 117-120.

Johnston, Roy J. "University of Miami: Learning and Instructional Resources Center," *Audiovisual Instruction*, Vol. 11, No. 2, February, 1966, pp. 91-93.

Karpisek, Marion E. "Media Centers: If You Can't Change the Design, Change the Rules," *American School and University*, Vol. 50, No. 10, June, 1978, pp. 54-55.

Klasing, Jane. "So You're Considering a Security System," *School Media Quarterly*, Vol. 7, No. 2, Winter, 1979, pp. 125-127.

Knirk, Frederick G. "Facilities for Learning," *Audiovisual Instruction*, Vol. 15, October, 1970, p. 33.

Kushing, Nolan. "Some Random Notes on Functional Design and Browsing Rooms," *American Libraries*, Vol. 7, February, 1976, pp. 92-95.

Laughlin, Mildred. "Action Activities," *Learning Today*, Vol. 10, No. 1, Winter, 1977, pp. 69-71.

LeClercq, Angie. "The AV Connection: Increasing Cooperation Between Classroom and Library," *Media and Methods*, Vol. 15, No. 9, May-June, 1979, pp. 34-37.

Likness, Craig S. "Information, Imagination, and the High School Library," *Clearing House*, Vol. 52, No. 9, May, 1979, pp. 416-418.

McAnulty, Laura. "Media-Based Learning Center," *Audiovisual Instruction*, Vol. 15, No. 2, February, 1970, pp. 50-54.

McCarthy, Patricia B. "Inservice at Eisenhower IMC: Helping Students Help Themselves," *Catholic Library World*, Vol. 49, No. 7, February, 1978, pp. 275-279.

McConeghy, Gary L. "School Building: A Plea for Logical Development," *Audiovisual Instruction*, Vol. 15, October, 1970, pp. 45-46.

McNerney, Mary Ellen. "The School Librarian and Public Relations: Showing That You Care," *Catholic Library World*, Vol. 50, No. 8, March, 1979, pp. 334-335.

Margrabe, Mary. "The Library Media Specialist and Total Curriculum Involvement," *Catholic Library World*, Vol. 49, No. 7, February, 1978, pp. 283-287.

Matlick, Richard. "A Learning Laboratory for the Small Community College," *Audiovisual Instruction*, Vol. 19, No. 7, September, 1974, pp. 30-32.

Menhusen, Bernadette *et al.* "Media Materials Center for the Severely Handicapped," *Journal of Special Education Technology*, Vol. 1, No. 2, July, 1978, pp. 5-12.

Merteus, J. "What Is a Resource Center?," *Educational Media International*, No. 4, 1975, pp. 6-8.

Miller, Hannah Elsa. "A Working Media Center: An All-Media Approach to Learning," *Audiovisual Instruction*, Vol. 19, No. 2, February, 1974, pp. 59-60.

Miller, Nancy. "Learning Resource Center—Its Role in Education," *Audiovisual Instruction*, Vol. 16, No. 5, May, 1971, pp. 48-49.

Miller, Robert E. "Teaching Skills in the Retrieval and Utilization of Materials and Equipment for Students and Faculty," *Catholic Library World*, Vol. 50, No. 8, March, 1979, pp. 327-329.

Moore, Nancy M. "Learning Centers: Turning on an Elementary Classroom," *Educational Technology*, Vol. 14, No. 11, November, 1974, pp. 24-26.

Offerman, Mary Columba, Sister. "The Instructional Media Center," *Clearing House*, Vol. 52, No. 2, October, 1978, pp. 61-64.

Olsen, Linda D. "Let's Redesign the Library," *Audiovisual Instruction*, Vol. 23, No. 5, May, 1978, pp. 41-42.

Olsen, Richard W. "How to Design a Science Learning Center," *Audiovisual Instruction*, Vol. 22, No. 3, March, 1977, pp. 48-51.

Paton, Bill. "School Libraries: The Librarian Is Responsible," *Library Association Record*, Vol. 79, No. 3, March, 1977, pp. 129-131.

Perelle, Ira. "Specifying the Instructional Media Center," *Educational Technology*, Vol. 19, No. 7, July, 1979, pp. 26-29.

Peterson, Gary T. "The Learning Center—A Second Time Around," *Audiovisual Instruction*, Vol. 19, No. 7, September, 1974, pp. 36-38.

Pileri, Iris. "Your Eye Witness Media Center—A Focus on Today's World," *Instructor*, Vol. 87, No. 9, April, 1978, pp. 84-89.

Polisky, Mildred. "Developing a Successful Business Skills Learning Center," *Audiovisual Instruction*, Vol. 21, No. 4, April, 1976, pp. 29-31.

Porter, D.S. "How to Design a Working IMC, Bridge School, Lexington, Mass.," *Educational Screen and Audiovisual Guide*, Vol. 46, November, 1967, p. 23.

Poston, Teresa G. "The Concept of the School Media Center and Its Services," *Peabody Journal of Education*, Vol. 55, No. 3, April, 1978, pp. 198-204.

Potter, Earl L., and G. Douglas Mayo. "Selection of Media by Media Centers," *Educational Technology*, Vol. 17, No. 4, April, 1977, pp. 45-48.

Randall, Warren. "School Facilities: AV Checklist," *Audiovisual Instruction*, Vol. 17, No. 10, December, 1973, pp. 16-17.

Rottman, Clara Thoren. "Media Services Enhanced Through Integrated Shelving," *School Media Quarterly*, Fall, 1976, pp. 23-30.

St. John, Walter D., and Margaret L. St. John. "Checklist for an LRC," *Audiovisual Instruction*, Vol. 21, No. 8, October, 1976, pp. 24-25.

Bibliography

Schmid, William T. "Is a Big Media Center a Big Problem?" *Audiovisual Instruction*, Vol. 21, No. 8, October, 1976, pp. 12-14.

Seager, Donald E. "Planning and Designing Media Facilities: The Don'ts and the Do's," *American School and University*, Vol. 50, No. 1, September, 1977, pp. 20, 22, 24.

Seager, Donald E. "Planning and Designing Media Facilities: Let's Consider Space," *American School and University*, Vol. 50, No. 6, February, 1978, pp. 50-51.

Seager, Donald E. "Planning and Designing Media Facilities: Let's Talk Space to Space," *American School and University*, Vol. 50, No. 8, April, 1978, pp. 30-31.

Seager, Donald E. "Planning and Designing Media Facilities: Let's Get Specific," *American School and University*, Vol. 50, No. 10, June, 1978, pp. 50-51.

Seager, Donald E. "Planning and Designing Media Facilities: Let's Furnish," *American School and University*, Vol. 50, No. 12, August, 1978, pp. 48-49.

Seager, Donald E. "Planning and Designing Media Facilities: Let's Lock Up," *American School and University*, Vol. 51, No. 2, October, 1978, pp. 58-59.

"Spiffing Up the Media Center," *Instructor*, Vol. 88, No. 2, September, 1978, pp. 82-86.

Stewart, Kent G. "Learning Spaces: Activities and Specifications," *Audiovisual Instruction*, Vol. 15, October, 1970, pp. 63-64.

Stroud, Janet G., and David G. Loertscher. "User Needs and School Library Service," *Catholic Library World*, Vol. 49, No. 4, November, 1977, pp. 162-165.

Vandergrift, Kay E. "Persons and Environment," *School Media Quarterly*, Vol. 4, No. 1, Fall, 1975, pp. 311-316.

Vandergrift, Kay E. "Selection: Reexamination and Reassessment," *School Media Quarterly*, Vol. 6, No. 2, Winter, 1978, pp. 103-111.

Vellerman, Keith A. "Library Adaptions for the Handicapped," *School Library Journal*, Vol. 21, No. 2, October, 1974, pp. 85-88.

Vollbrecht, John. "Will Future Media Centers Be Built Around Computers?" *Audiovisual Instruction*, Vol. 19, No. 5, May, 1974, pp. 42-44.

Weber, Mack. "Back to Basics: Its Meaning for School Media Programs," *School Library Journal*, Vol. 24, No. 2, October, 1977, pp. 83-85.

Wilkinson, Gene L. "Managers Are More Than Just Administrators," *Audiovisual Instruction*, Vol. 23, No. 7, October, 1978, pp. 20-21.

Wood, Johanna S. "Media Programs in Open Space Schools," *School Media Quarterly*, Vol. 4, No. 3, Spring, 1976, pp. 205, 214.

Wools, Blanche. "School Library Media Programs and Services for Youth," *Catholic Library World*, Vol. 50, No. 5, December, 1978, pp. 200-204.

Wright, John G. "Evaluating Materials for Children and Young Adults," *Canadian Library Journal*, Vol. 35, No. 6, December, 1978, pp. 439-441.

Wyman, Raymond. "The Resourceteria Concept," *Audiovisual Instruction*, Vol. 19, No. 3, March, 1973, pp. 23-24.

About the Author

LaMond F. Beatty is Associate Professor in the department of Educational Systems and Learning Resources, Graduate School of Education, University of Utah, Salt Lake City, Utah. Dr. Beatty has taught at the University of Utah since 1961. Along with his teaching responsibilities, Professor Beatty has been Assistant Director and Director (1961 through 1973) of the Educational Media Center for the University of Utah, helping to develop the Center from a small 16mm film rental and campus service agency to a Media Center that offers a 16mm film, photographic, and graphic service plus an instructional design unit utilized by instructors and administrators in all colleges of the University of Utah.

Professor Beatty has published widely, including magazine articles, monographs, textbook chapters, manuals, independent study courses, and mini-textbooks.

Dr. Beatty maintains affiliations with both local and national professional organizations, including the Utah Educational Media Association (UEMA), the Utah Library Association (ULA), the Association for Educational Communications and Technology (AECT), Phi Delta Kappa, the American Library Association (ALA), and the Consortium of University Film Libraries.